Rhinegold Study Guides

A Student's Guide
to AS Drama and Theatre
Studies

for the **Edexcel** Specification

by

Max Harvey and Nigel Williams

R·

Rhinegold Publishing Ltd
241 Shaftesbury Avenue
London WC2H 8TF
Telephone: 01832 270333
Fax: 01832 275560
www.rhinegold.co.uk

Rhinegold Drama and Theatre Studies Study Guides
A Student's Guide to AS Drama and Theatre Studies for the Edexcel Specification
A Student's Guide to A2 Drama and Theatre Studies for the Edexcel Specification

A Student's Guide to AS Drama and Theatre Studies for the AQA Specification
A Student's Guide to A2 Drama and Theatre Studies for the AQA Specification

Rhinegold Performance Studies Study Guides
A Student's Guide to AS Performance Studies for the OCR Specification
A Student's Guide to A2 Performance Studies for the OCR Specification

Other Rhinegold Study Guides
Students' Guides to GCSE, AS and A2 Music for the AQA, Edexcel and OCR Specifications
Listening Tests for Students for the AQA, Edexcel and OCR GCSE and A Level Music Specifications
A Student's Guide to Music Technology for the Edexcel AS and A2 Specification
Listening Tests for Students for the Edexcel AS and A2 Music Technology Specification
A Student's Guide to GCSE Music for the WJEC Specification
Students' Guides to AS and A2 Religious Studies for the AQA, Edexcel and OCR Specifications

Rhinegold Publishing also publishes Classical Music, Classroom Music, Early Music Today, Music Teacher, Opera Now, Piano, The Singer, British and International Music Yearbook, British Performing Arts Yearbook, Music Education Yearbook, Rhinegold Dictionary of Music in Sound.

First published 2004 in Great Britain by
Rhinegold Publishing Ltd
241 Shaftesbury Avenue
London WC2H 8TF
Telephone: 01832 270333
Fax: 01832 275560
www.rhinegold.co.uk
© Rhinegold Publishing Ltd
Reprinted 2005

You should always check the current requirements of the examination, since these may change.
Copies of the Edexcel Specification may be obtained from
Edexcel Publications, Adamsway, Mansfield, Notts NG18 4FN
Telephone: 01623 467467, Email: publications@linneydirect.com
See also the Edexcel website at www.edexcel.org.uk

A Student's Guide to AS Drama and Theatre Studies for the Edexcel Specification
British Library Cataloguing in Publication Data.
A catalogue record for this book is available from the British Library.

ISBN 1-904226-28-0

Printed in Great Britain by WPG Ltd

Contents

The authors

Max Harvey was head of drama at Wellsway School for nine years before becoming head of year in the sixth form. He has been responsible for establishing drama within the school's curriculum and developing schemes of work and assessment structures for all key stages. He studied drama at Exeter University before completing his teacher training at Bretton Hall. Max has worked in an advisory capacity for the education department of the Theatre Royal Bath and is on the board of directors. More recently, he has contributed to books on the role of citizenship within the school curriculum.

Nigel Williams has been director of drama at Gordonstoun School for seven years. He has been teaching drama and theatre for 20 years in a variety of schools ranging from an inner-city comprehensive to a rural upper school. Nigel trained at Bristol University and St Paul's teacher-training college in Cheltenham, and he studied drama in education at Leicester University. He also trained in mime and physical theatre at the London City Institute. He has directed numerous school productions and as director of Bedfordshire Youth Theatre 1986–1996 he commissioned and produced new plays as well as traditional, contemporary and musical texts. He was an Associated Examining Board examiner for A-level theatre studies for eight years and is currently a team leader for Edexcel on AS drama and theatre studies. He has also been responsible for the in-service training of drama teachers in Bedfordshire.

The editors

Emma Whale (project manager), Charlotte Regan (assistant editor), Joanna Hughes (designer), Lucien Jenkins (editor).

Acknowledgements

In the writing of a guide such as this many people have contributed. The authors and publishers are grateful to the following people for their specific advice, support and expert contributions: Tim Armitage, Hallam Bannister, Emma Findlow, Luke Harley, Nicola Harvey, Laura Hobbs, John Nicol, Danny Parker, Alan Perks, Andrew Psirides, Andy Thomas, Abigail Walmsley, Jonathan Wikeley and Justine Williams. The authors are also conscious of having drawn on a lifetime's reading. More recently, the growth in use of the Internet has made an unparalleled amount of exciting information and challenging opinion widely available. Although every attempt has been made to acknowledge both the primary and secondary sources drawn on, it is impossible to do justice to the full range of material that has shaped the creation of this book. The authors would therefore like to apologise if anyone's work has not been properly acknowledged. They would be happy to hear from authors or publishers so that any such errors or omissions may be rectified in future editions.

Introduction

Drama appeals to our instinct. The act of producing theatre appears to stem from a natural human desire to create and perform. Stories have always been told, events recounted, rituals celebrated – and the variety of styles that exists in modern theatre reflects the power of an art form that has been evolving over thousands of years. It is a vibrant subject that is very much alive and will continue to grow during your time on the course. We would hope that you have chosen to study drama and theatre studies at AS level because you have a keen interest in certain elements of the theatrical process. Whether you have been involved as actor, designer, director or audience member, you will have started to form opinions on what you like and dislike. This personal response is vital if you are going to succeed. You need to learn to trust your instinct while developing your understanding of theatre through performance, observation and research.

Why drama?

This guide is intended to provide assistance to students of Edexcel AS drama and theatre studies. What is offered here is extra help with your course, rather than a substitute for what your teachers have to offer: you're still going to need to go to your lessons. This guide will take you through the various elements of the course and explain the precise requirements of each unit, identifying what the examiners are looking for, while offering advice and suggestions for practical activities. It is important to remember that this is a performance-based subject.

The majority of the work will rely on you working closely with other members of your class. You will need to be open and honest, while recognising the importance of compromising your individual ideas in order to ensure group success. Throughout the book, we shall be offering ideas for practical work for you to experiment with in lessons. These exercises will enable you to recognise each person's strengths and allow you to learn from each other. Drama and theatre studies is possibly the only subject you will be taking where the end result is dependent on the work of the whole group. In order to be successful you will need to work well as a team. All theatres rely on this philosophy and it is only right that this is reflected in how you are assessed during the course.

Teamwork

As you study the subject, you will gain an improved understanding of the potential of the written text. You will encounter several different plays that cover a range of genres, and you will learn how to interpret the words in performance and evaluate their possible impact on an audience. In this guide, there is advice on how to approach specific plays, but many of these ideas can be applied to any text from any period. You should look to draw comparisons, link ideas to other theatrical practitioners and consequently develop your command of production techniques.

The theatrical process

This is a course that relies on the group working together but a good student will look to extend their knowledge with independent research. Use the suggested tasks as a starting point for your work. Pursue some of the ideas for wider reading. Get excited by the possibilities of live theatre. If you do this, you will provide yourself with an excellent foundation for tackling all aspects of the course.

The AS modules

Unit 1: Exploration of drama and theatre (30%)

In this unit, you will study two different plays. You will be taught about the original performance conditions and the concepts that influenced the playwrights when they were writing the text. You will look closely at the structure of each play and the different techniques that are used in order to create meaning. Use this information to find other plays, directors or theatre companies that may have influenced or been influenced by the plays you are studying. This will help you to gain an appreciation of the genre and a wider understanding of the plays in a social, cultural and historical context.

Your understanding of the text should be reinforced through a series of practical workshops, which will enable you to understand the dramatic potential of the text. You will also record your investigations in a portfolio, called your Exploration Notes. These notes may include drawings and diagrams as well as written work. Your teacher will be assessing your contribution throughout the workshops and your mark for the unit will be based equally on this practical work as well as your Exploration Notes.

Unit 2: Text in performance (40%)

During this unit you will participate in the production of a play. The script may be similar in style to those studied in unit 1, or it may require you to gain an understanding of another genre.

You can choose to be assessed on different theatrical skills. If you opt for performing, you will be marked on your acting ability. Obviously, you will have lines to learn and you will need to think about how you can create a role that will reflect your dramatic skill and understanding. You will be directed by your teacher, who will give you advice on how to develop the character successfully, but ultimately the responsibility for the performance lies with you.

Alternatively you can focus on design skills, opting for one or more of the following areas: lighting, set and props, costume, mask and make-up, sound. Each skill will need to be supported by a portfolio of research and a final design linked to one of the plays being performed.

An external examiner will assess you, and you will be marked on your interpretation, technical ability and communication of the meaning of the text.

Unit 3: Text in context (30%)

This is a written exam, split into two distinct sections. The first links to your work in unit 2, in your role as either performer or designer. You will need to answer three short questions based on your experiences during rehearsals and performance. Each question will focus on a specific element and will ask for a personal response to the process with suggestions on how the work might have been improved. During your initial work on the play you should have kept notes on the development of ideas (Context Summary Notes). These can be taken into the examination and can be used as reference when writing your response.

The second section tests your ability to appreciate live theatre. You will see several theatrical performances and you will need to learn how to form a critical interpretation of the work. Your thoughts on the performers, designers and directors can be recorded in note form (Performance Analysis Notes) and used in the examination. In addition to this, you should consider the social, cultural and historical context in which the play was originally performed and its effectiveness as a contemporary production.

Each section carries equal marks and the exam lasts two hours.

Understanding Theatre

What is this chapter for?

One of the many exciting aspects of theatre is its variety. The evolution of formal performance during the last 2,500 years has led to an incredible array of performance styles. Many are deeply rooted in humankind's instinctive desire to create and perform. The joy of this AS-level course is that you are free to explore as many of these styles as you wish. Of course, there are guidelines that will be set by both the exam board and your teacher, but within these there is real freedom for you to explore.

It would be impossible to outline or even attempt to define each of the styles that have existed within the context of this book. Nor will you be expected to refer to them all in any of the assessment tasks. The aim is for you to develop an interest in theatre, and to consider how any performance could have been influenced by other plays, practitioners or events in the world. There are few right answers. Yes, there are key terms that need to be understood and used appropriately, but you will succeed in this course if you keep your mind open.

The focus of this course is on practical understanding. You will be assessed either on your performance or design skills, and your ability to analyse and reflect on the work of others. Therefore, it is important that you have a sound understanding of different theatre styles, of how these affect concepts of design and of the terminology needed to give an informed analysis during the written elements.

You will not be examined directly on the information in this chapter – concerning key practitioners, design ideas and important terminology. Rather, you can use this opening chapter as a starting-point to the course and as a point of reference as you progress through the modules. Experiment with the ideas practically and spend time researching those that you find most interesting. This will enable you to create your own understanding of theatre which will help you to respond to all of the tasks in a confident and informed way.

Rehearsing theatre: Stanislavski

His surname was actually Alekseyev; he adopted Stanislavski as a stage name.

Konstantin Sergeyevich Stanislavski (1863–1938) is often considered to be the father of modern theatre, as he provided a rehearsal system that allowed actors to create characters in which they – and an audience – could believe. He was born in Russia and took part in his first performance when he was just seven. His privileged upbringing enabled him to experience a variety of theatre forms, and when he was 14 his father converted an outbuilding on their estate into a well-equipped performance space.

The dominant forms at the time were opera, farce and melodrama, in which the entertainment relied on stock characters. The acting was almost mechanical, with physical movements superficially repeated in order to convey clichéd emotion (for example, a hand placed on the heart represented love). Rehearsals – when they occurred – were formulaic in style and rigidly structured to save time and expense. There was hardly any exploration of character. Actors would move over to a window or fireplace because they always did, this was standard procedure. There was direct communication with the audience, rather than with the other characters: actors would face the front for the most part and the set would be arranged around such action. Costumes were based on what was available, with certain actors preferring to keep the same outfit from one performance to the next.

Despite this, Stanislavski quickly became fascinated by the art of acting. On rare occasions he encountered people who had real presence. They were able to convey a physical truth that allowed him to truly believe in the character. This was something that he admired and sought to emulate. He tried copying their mannerisms in an attempt to recreate their power on stage. Initially he was extremely unsuccessful but ironically this became his real strength. His passion for acting perfection and his search for a sense of realism helped him to develop a system which is commonly used today.

In 1897, Stanislavski co-founded the Moscow Arts Theatre and established a clear set of ideals that needed to be maintained in all productions. The company was to be based on ensemble acting: actors would be expected to alternate between large and small roles. The style of performance had to be clear and sensitive, detailed and truthful. The set and costume needed to be intricate and had to be redesigned for every production. The highest standards were expected at all times.

Stanislavski's search for a new style of acting is extremely well documented. He wrote three books as a guide to his system: *An Actor Prepares*, *Building a Character* and *Creating a Role*. Each of these is clearly structured and easy to read. They are written from the perspective of a young actor, Kostya, who is desperately trying to improve his skill. He attends classes with the fictitious director Tortsov, who leads him through a range of experiences that help him to understand the art of acting. This master-student format is extremely effective and allows Stanislavski an endearing medium for presenting common mistakes or obsessions without sounding patronising or judgemental.

During the next few pages we will explore many of his ideas through a practical format. The aim is to provide you with a series of tools that you can use during the rehearsal process when preparing your chosen piece for performance.

Stimulating the desire to create

Unlike his contemporaries, Stanislavski placed real emphasis on the importance of the rehearsal. The actors needed to examine each text,

Stock characters

One of Stanislavski's key influences was the actor Mikhail Shchepkin (1788–1863), who believed the actor should 'crawl under the skin of the character'. *Stanislavski: an introduction by Jean Benedetti* (Methuen 1982).

Moscow Art Theatre

Key texts

An Actor Prepares (Methuen 1980), *Building a Character* (Methuen 1979) and *Creating a Role* (Methuen 1998).

they needed to explore the characters and the performances needed to be organic, adapting to the unique circumstances of each night.

However, in order to create, he realised that there was a need to ensure actors were focused and committed to the work, without any of the baggage of the outside world. Exercises became an essential element of an actor's training. Some were general, appropriate for anyone at any time. Others were more specific off-text work, where the improvisation or discussion might directly feedback into the creation of a role.

Try some of the following general exercises as a way into your rehearsals:

This activity is in several stages.

Begin by walking around the room touching different objects and calling out their names, for example: chair, wall, clock. Now, walking again, try calling out the name of the object that you previously touched. So, as you touch the wall shout 'chair', as you touch the clock shout 'wall'. If you are feeling confident, try naming the object touched two turns before (when you touch the clock shout 'chair'). This exercise warms up your mind and helps you to forget about other thoughts. It also helps to settle nerves as people laugh at their inability to remember the names of simple objects.

Get into pairs. Stand opposite your partner. Stare at each other and take it in turns to say a number in the following sequence: 1, 2, 3, 1, 2, 3, 1 ... and so on. Try to say the numbers as fast as possible. This task sounds easy but try it: it's amazing how hard it is to count! If you feel comfortable with this exercise, try the following variations:

➢ Whenever you say 1, tap your head with your left hand

➢ Whenever you say 3, stamp your right foot

➢ Alternate your movement so both hands and feet are used

➢ Try removing the number 1 but maintain the action

➢ Remove the number 3 and maintain the action.

This is an excellent way of stimulating your mind. The concept appears so easy but your brain finds it difficult. This is similar to acting. What could appear simpler than being yourself on stage? This apparent contradiction is something that obsessed Stanislavski during his life. Try the following exercise, which is based on a section in *An Actor Prepares*.

Ask four members of your group to leave the rehearsal space. While they are outside, hide an object in the room (Stanislavski used a pin in a curtain). Send one person outside to explain to the volunteers what they need to find. State that it is a competition; the first person to find it will win a prize. They are free to talk and even distract others. Once they are clear about the activity, they can enter. Watch how they search and monitor any use of sound. When the object is found, explain that they need simply to repeat the exercise, exactly as they have just performed it.

Usually, the second version will be a lot less convincing. The object should still be hidden in the same place and therefore it is extremely difficult to act the search as convincingly. This is why Stanislavski's system is so useful, as it gives you practical solutions to these problems. Try repeating the exercise when you have finished reading through the ideas in this chapter. Hopefully, you should find it a lot easier to recreate the scene.

Given circumstances

As a way of preventing his actors from relying on stock characters, Stanislavski put real emphasis on the specific nature of each play. He expected his company to explore what he called the 'given circumstances' of each text in an attempt to find the subtle nuances in the writing, the complexities of the script. The given circumstances can be defined most simply as the facts that cannot be changed by the actor, anything over which they have no control. Rather than discarding an action by saying 'my character wouldn't do this', performers were told to base their role on the specific information the playwright has given them. Examples of such given circumstances include the story of the play, the events within it, the period and place in which it's set, and the director's and designer's interpretations. Essentially, any facts about the world of the play that are given directly or that could be deduced needed to be noted. This would be the starting point of any work on the text.

Choose a play with which you are familiar and identify the given circumstances. If you saw it as a production, try to distinguish between the facts provided by the playwright and the interpretation of the director. Compare this list with another member of your group or with discussions of the play on the Internet.

As a way of exploring the play, Stanislavski applied the concept of the Magic IF – in which the actors were encouraged to believe in the circumstances no matter how fantastic they may have been. The actor needs to ask himself the question, 'If I were this person, how would I feel?' This ensures each role is deeply rooted in the facts of the play. In the later stages of his work, Stanislavski changed this concept to 'What would I *do*?' as he developed a new emphasis on physical action (see page 16).

However, it would be wrong to assume that all essential information is supplied by the playwright. In fact, in some plays, a lot of questions are left unanswered. Therefore, the actor needs to supplement the information with their imagination in order to 'create the moments between the scenes – the flow and continuity between the character's life'. When a character leaves the stage, where do they go? If an off-stage conversation is referred to in the script, improvise what happened. This will help to create the complete picture. Magic IF acts as a key here: by asking themselves what they would do in a particular situation, the actor unlocks their own imagination, creating actions that are true to themselves and thus believable to an audience.

" The investigation of the script, the clear understanding of its nature and its relation to an actor's own experience is the primary process in rehearsal from which all else follows. "

Stanislavski: an introduction by Jean Benedetti (Methuen 1982)

Magic IF

" IF acts as a lever to lift us out of the world of actuality into the realm of imagination. "

Stanislavski, *An Actor Prepares*, trans. E. Hapgood (Methuen 1980)

Imagination

Benedetti, *Stanislavski: an introduction by Jean Benedetti* (Methuen 1982).

Find a partner and act out the following: A is a friend who has agreed to meet B at the bus stop before going on to the cinema. B is late because they have just witnessed an accident in which a car and a young cyclist collided. Improvise the scene with A being quite frustrated and B reluctant to talk.

Once you have come to a natural end, try running the scene again but this time each individual needs to be clear about the circumstances. A needs to consider how often B has been late in the past. Do they often go to the cinema? What else was A considering doing that evening? B needs to imagine the specifics of the accident and how they felt at the scene. Did they come directly from the accident or did something else happen? Each of these facts should help to create a more complete picture and consequently a more believable scene.

Units and objectives

When acting, have you ever been daunted by the length of a scene? Have you ever been conscious of making mistakes because you were thinking about what was approaching rather than the section you were working on?

Realistic scenes are often extremely complex. Characters' emotions can vary tremendously and yet tension within a scene can be reliant on the briefest of exchanges within the heart of some lengthy dialogue. Stanislavski believed that in order to create a successful performance, each scene should be subdivided into units, with a new unit beginning whenever there is a change in the psychological state of the character. These breaks could be as short as a word or encompass the whole scene, depending on the play. They are identified by the actor and director and used as temporary divisions while working on the text.

Each character in each unit is given an objective. This is always in the form of an active verb and the phrase 'I want …' – it contains within it the germ of an action that will drive the scene forwards. Quite simply, it is the character's intention for the extract and should be the dominant force behind all thought and movement.

Eventually the actor should be able to connect all the units together in order to decide what the character's main objective is for the whole play. This is the **superobjective** – an overall focus that motivates the character throughout the play.

Tip

Objectives should always be positive. Phrases such as 'I don't want to be here' don't help the actor. The focus needs to be on what the character *wants* to do.

 Ask one member of your group to enter the room, having decided on an objective, and sit on a chair facing the audience. They could think of their own or try experimenting with any of the following:

➢ I want to control my feelings

➢ I want revenge

➢ I want to forget what I've just done

➢ I want to be alone.

Decide on a location for the scene, perhaps the lounge of their parents' house. Add another character to the scene and give them a conflicting objective. This will act as an obstacle within the scene and create tension.

Arrange your group in a circle and put one chair in the middle. Ask a volunteer to sit on it. The aim is simple. Someone from the circle (A) has to improvise a scene with the person sat in the centre (B). A's objective is 'I want the person in the middle to get off the chair'. B needs to accept the given circumstances of any scene they are given and they must be careful not to block the action. All behaviour must be as realistic as possible.

The actions of other characters can hinder an objective. These are referred to as **obstacles**.

The best way of understanding how the technique works is by applying the ideas directly to the text. Look at the following unit from *The Cherry Orchard* by Anton Chekhov and apply objectives to it based on the given circumstances.

Chekhov, *The Cherry Orchard*, trans. Michael Frayn (Methuen Theatre Classics 1978).

Given circumstances:
Dunyasha is a chambermaid who romanticises her life and fancies herself. She is in her late teens and has airs above her station. Yasha is in his twenties. He has just come back from Paris, is arrogant and is affected with an extremely high opinion of himself. He is a womaniser.
The unit is set in the nursery of a country mansion. The occasion is a family gathering to greet returning relatives. There is much coming and going.

Comments	Text
How much of the stage space does Yasha cross?	Enter Yasha with a rug and travelling bag
At what point does she recognise him?	YASHA: (*crosses with delicacy*) All right to come through?
	DUNYASHA: I shouldn't even recognise you, Yasha. You've changed so abroad!
	YASHA: Mm… And who are you?
	DUNYASHA: When you left I was so high… (*Indicates from the floor.*) Dunyasha. Fyodor Kozoyedov's daughter. You don't remember!
Is she surprised? Offended?	YASHA: Mm… Quite a pippin, aren't you? (*Looks round and embraces her. She screams and breaks a saucer.*)
Is Yasha's comment a compliment or is it patronising? Is the dropping of the saucer an accident or does she do it for attention?	Exit Yasha swiftly

Subtext

In most realistic plays, the spoken dialogue contains a subtext – a meaning beneath the text. Awareness of this was crucial to the development of Stanislavski's theatre and prevented his actors from drifting into the two-dimensional performances of the past. It was no longer possible simply to copy the physical actions of other actors or attempt to recreate their vocal tones. The external portrayal needed to be backed up with an internal, intellectual response. The performance became a personal interpretation based on an actor's own experience and instinct.

This concept needs to be remembered when tackling all scripts, since there is a tendency to play scenes at their face value. However, the script has been carefully written by the playwright, with words chosen for maximum impact and it is vital that you search for alternative interpretations, reading between the lines.

" The printed words do not contain the full meaning, as in purely literary forms. They depend on what lies beneath them. "

Stanislavski: an introduction by Jean Benedetti, (Methuen 1982).

With a partner, act the following dialogue at face value:

> A: I'm sorry.
>
> B: Really?
>
> A: You know you can trust me.
>
> B: Thanks.

Repeat the scene experimenting each time with more complex characterisation. What could the given circumstances be here? Perhaps B is a husband who has recently cheated on A, his wife. Or is it the other way around? Imagine all the possible subtexts that could be underneath this simple extract.

In a group of three, improvise the following scene.

It is lunch time and three friends are discussing their food. All of their dialogue must be related to the food they are eating but one member of the group has a crush on one of the others, and must reveal this subtext through their vocal and physical work. If acted well, the scene will be funny but the dialogue in itself will appear quite basic. This should highlight to you the value of subtext.

Emotion memory

If an actor is to engage intellectually with their role, then they should also look to connect emotionally. Personal experience is essential when attempting to convey a truthful performance and all actors should strive to learn how to harness past events in order to feed into the detail of their role.

The key to these feelings is in the senses, since they have the power to stimulate the past. Imagining the smell of home cooking can create a sense of calm. The sound of the sea might stimulate romantic thoughts. The sight and feel of a busy street could create anxiety. Using your own memory bank to create truthful actions on stage is not an exercise to be treated lightly: it is an intensely personal experience and may take time. In this sense, it is more a private rehearsal technique.

> " Since you are still capable of blushing or growing pale at the recollection of an experience, since you still fear to recall a certain tragic happening, we can conclude that you possess an emotion memory. "
>
> Stanislavski, *An Actor Prepares*, trans. E. Hapgood (Methuen 1980)

Think of a moment when you were clearly embarrassed. Try to recreate that emotion by considering the circumstances and how they affected your senses.

Stanislavski acknowledged that emotions were a difficult tool to harness and could at times result in imposing an incorrect intensity of feeling onto a script. As he modified his ideas, he realised the emphasis needed to come from action. The actor is looking for the correct physical reaction to the emotion conjured up. To find this physical action, you need to conjure up the emotion through remembering the small details of the moment. For example, remembering the first time you fell in love is unlikely to provide you with much physical information. But by remembering the details (the smells, where you were, the music that might have been playing) you should be able to build up the overall memory and remember your physical reaction at that time.

Circle of attention and public solitude

In the Russian theatre of Stanislavski's time, gestures were bold, voices were loud and characterisation was unsubtle. The performance was aimed directly at the audience, who could sit back and be entertained by the spectacle. Stanislavski was appalled by the false nature of such work and insisted that his actors should not be distracted by the 'black hole' of the audience. They needed to create an imaginary fourth wall, a barrier between themselves and the auditorium, with their point of focus always on the stage. This would help to embody the philosophy of ensemble acting, where the focus was not on one star actor, but the company as a whole.

As a way of emphasising this idea, each actor was asked to imagine himself or herself within a small pool of light. This was referred to as a 'circle of attention' and had the effect of focusing the performer's mind on the smallest of details and drawing the audience into the action. The effect is similar to the image of a solitary child playing with a toy. Their focus on their own world of play is immense and as an onlooker you can often become hypnotised by their actions, imagining what they must be thinking. Stanislavski referred to this effect as 'public solitude': despite sharing a space and being observed by a large group of people, you are able to convey a sense of true isolation.

> In such a small space you can use your concentrated attention to examine various objects in most intricate details, and also to carry on more complicated activities such as defining shades of feeling and thought.
>
> Stanislavski, *An Actor Prepares*, trans. E. Hapgood (Methuen 1980)

In a small group, ask for one volunteer to act in front of the others. The performer should have a small object to focus on, such as a box of matches, a bunch of keys, a ring. Without talking they need to improvise a scene that suggests an emotional reaction to the object. As an audience, try to pinpoint what skills are used in order to convey the mood of the scene. Are you interested in the action? Which elements of the performance are most successful?

This intense level of concentration is essential in developing a well-rounded character. Think about yourself for a moment and where you focus your attention. Essentially, you focus on three different areas – another person, an object or yourself. This may appear quite obvious, but in terms of creating a believable character on stage, your concentration can often wander to other things: When do I move? Why isn't the audience laughing? What's my next line?

Communion

From this, Stanislavski developed the notion of communion, which is an unspoken language on stage. He said that actors must at all times have communion with something or someone: it is only by maintaining an uninterrupted exchange of feelings and actions between the characters on stage that an audience's attention can be held. He explained how this was to work by asking his actors to visualise rays coming out from their eyes and fingertips that must always be in constant connection with someone or something. Stanislavski searched for an intimate performance and used small rehearsal spaces to help him create the desired effect.

> "Exterior action, movement, gesture were reduced to almost nothing. The actors were required to 'radiate' their feelings, to do everything through their eyes, by tiny changes in tone and inflection. To 'commune' with each other."
>
> *Stanislavski: an introduction by Jean Benedetti* (Methuen 1982)

The concept of intense concentration and discipline in performance is relatively easy to grasp but practically it is a lot more difficult to maintain.

 In a group of three, try to recreate the following situation in stages, focusing on another character, an object or yourself:

➢ A enters and sees an envelope under a chair. They look inside, see there is a letter and read it. It is addressed to B and is written by C. C writes how they hate B's attitude, how B appears to victimise C viciously at every opportunity. A, having read the note, puts it back in the envelope. Pause the scene at this point. Ask A how easy it was to maintain their focus. Were the audience drawn into the performance?

➢ Repeat the scene but this time carry it on with A trying to replace the letter under the chair as B enters and wonders what A is doing. B's reaction should indicate that they haven't seen the letter. Improvise the dialogue, making the object a focus for both characters at certain points. Pause once again and discuss whether it became more difficult to retain the focus with two actors on stage.

➢ Repeat the action once again leading up to B insisting on seeing the letter. At this point C should enter looking for the letter that has dropped from their pocket. C sees the letter in B's hand. Improvise. When the scene comes to a natural conclusion, discuss the action and the use of communion.

The method of physical action

Stanislavski's early concern with recreating truthful emotions through intellectual exercises was modified as he matured and developed as an actor and director. He became concerned that some aspects of his system, such as emotion memory, were not only complex but perhaps even emotionally dangerous for an actor to undergo. He realised that there was a need for balance between internal and external action. After all, physical activity is inextricably linked to mental thought. Many of us learn better when we are active. If you have lost your keys, you may have tried pacing round the house as a way of reminding yourself where you left them. So, as an actor, it is vital to use both elements in the generation of a truthful performance.

Tempo-rhythm

Stanislavski became interested in the unique pace of movement as related to emotion, and came to stress the importance of finding an inner rhythm for a character. If you can find the correct rhythm for an action, you are likely to generate an emotional response as believable as those discovered through emotion memory.

Get into pairs. Person A should walk around the room as he or she naturally would, while person B observes. After a minute, B walks behind A, copying their walk exactly. B should note the positioning of the arms, how the head is held and the change in weight and balance when A turns corners. After a minute, A moves away while B tries to maintain A's walk. Repeat the exercise with B being observed. You should note the uniqueness of each person's walk and how different it can make you feel inside.

This link between the physical and the mental is quite difficult to grasp but is an extremely useful acting tool. Benedetti manages to summarise the theory in quite a succinct way:

> Within the action of the play events, emotions have a particular pulse and pattern to them. Tempo, as in music, denotes the speed of an action or feeling – fast, slow, medium. Rhythm internally indicates the intensity with which an emotion is experienced; externally it indicates the patterns of gesture, moves and actions which express the emotion.

The simplest way of imagining this concept is by placing yourself in a position in which you do not want your physicality to portray how you are feeling emotionally. If you are going for a job, your inner nerves might be hidden by an external calm. Consequently your internal rhythm would be high but your external gestures might be small. This intricate detail helps to ensure an extremely complex understanding of character and hopefully a more sophisticated portrayal.

Stanislavski: an introduction by Jean Benedetti (Methuen 1982).

Rehearsing theatre: Brecht

Bertolt Brecht (1898–1956) played a huge part in influencing modern theatre as we know it today, and you will be employing many of his ideas, theories and practices in the way you work on this course without realising it. He was a playwright, a director (of his own plays and those of other people) and author of a good deal of commentary on how theatre should be created. His theories changed during his lifetime, and were not fully realised in all the plays he wrote, but many of them support much of what he was trying to communicate.

Life and background

Brecht was born in Augsburg, Germany in 1898 and lived there until the early 1920s. He was born into a fairly affluent family and studied medicine at the University of Munich before returning to Augsburg and serving in an army hospital during the first world war.

During this time, he developed an anti-war sentiment in response to the horrors he saw in the hospitals. Married to this was an anti-bourgeois attitude that reflected his anger and frustration at the way society had experienced war and dealt with its aftermath, as well as an interest in Marxism as a way forward for the financially and politically unstable Germany. He also developed an interest in the movement in art and literature known as Expressionism.

In order to escape the parochial society of Augsburg, Brecht moved to Munich, and soon after that to Berlin. Here he began the second phase of his writing, his *Lehrstücke*, or 'learning plays', in which he started to explore the ideas of epic theatre and the notion of instruction through plays. During this time he became a fully-fledged Marxist and spoke out against the Nazi party.

In 1933, he was forced to go into exile to escape the Nazis, and he fled to Switzerland and then Denmark before eventually travelling to the USA. He did some film work in Hollywood but always felt

> " No one seriously concerned with the theatre can bypass Brecht. Brecht is the key figure of our time, and all theatre work today at some point starts or returns to his statements and achievements. "
>
> Peter Brook, *An Empty Stage* 1969

Further study

Using the Internet, an encyclopedia or the resources of your school's history department, find out more about what happened to Germany after the conclusion of the first world war. See *below* for more on Expressionism.

uncomfortable there because of his communist roots. In Nazi Germany his work was reviled, his books destroyed and his citizenship withdrawn. It was during this time in exile that he wrote most of his great plays, further developing the idea of epic theatre.

In 1949 Brecht returned to a divided Germany where he formed his own company, the Berliner Ensemble. He was looked on with suspicion in capitalist West Germany because of his political stance, and also in communist East Germany due to his unorthodox theories. His contributions to theatre and his significance as a theatre practitioner were eventually recognised in the 1950s. Brecht died of a heart attack in 1956.

Influences

Brecht dedicated himself to creating a new way of thinking about and using theatre. In his quest for the new, however, he borrowed much from the past and present to help shape his ideas.

Expressionism

Expressionism was a movement in literature and art that originated in Germany before the first world war and ended in the 1920s. It tried to destroy superficial ideas of reality and explore the deeper meanings underneath. It stood for all things erratic and explosive over the smooth and linear. The resulting works of art appear distorted, and sometimes even tortured and grotesque.

Playwrights of the time writing in this style were affected by feelings of anger and despair at the state of society, particularly since the war, and the content of their plays reflect their attitude towards the values of society and the idea of capitalism. Many of the characters within the plays were reduced to titles to represent these concepts.

> In the play *Gas* by Georg Kaiser, for example, the characters include: the Engineer, the Girl, the Gentleman In White.

 There were also Expressionist films, most famously Fritz Lang's *Metropolis* (1926). Try to get hold of a copy of the film and watch it. See how it uses camera angles and editing to fragment the linear nature of the film and distort the reality of the story.

Brecht ultimately rejected Expressionism because he felt it relied too heavily on the irrational. However, Expressionism certainly influenced the way he tried to get audiences thinking about stories and theatre with a new perspective; the way he fragmented the line of his stories and created episodes; and the way he treated the characters of his plays (in that they were often archetypes and represented types of people).

Marxism

Brecht took much from the communist writing of Karl Marx (1818–1883), in terms of his hatred of capitalism, his anti-militarist views, his sense of justice and injustice, and his understanding of the importance of history. These ideas and principles became very apparent within the content of his plays.

> Although always sympathetic to communism, Brecht never became a member of the Communist party.

Other writers

Brecht was accused of plagiarism during his life, as many of his ideas for stories were borrowed from other writers such as Maxim Gorky, Christopher Marlowe, Sophocles and William Shakespeare.

But Brecht was always borrowing to re-invent and not just replicate. It wasn't just narrative and content that he used – he also borrowed form and structure ideas. The play *Woyzeck* by Georg Büchner influenced Brecht in terms of themes, but more importantly showed Brecht how to use unconnected scenes, which was the beginning of his idea of montage. The way in which Shakespeare used characters to comment on the action through use of Prologue and Epilogue, and the way in which the characters used the conventions of theatre language, such as the aside and soliloquy, also showed Brecht the potential for controlling the audience's response.

Brecht was also very interested in other world theatre forms. Watching the famous Chinese actor Mei La Fang perform in Moscow in 1935 without make-up, costume or lighting made Brecht realise that an audience would accept the fiction of theatre without a production having to cause them to 'suspend their disbelief'. This had a tremendous influence on the way he presented his work to the audience, the way he worked with his actors and the way that he staged his and others' plays.

His concern for the theatre's relationship with the audience also led to his interest in sporting events, particularly boxing. Brecht wanted theatre to have the same universal appeal and be equally popular. He really wanted theatre to learn from the relationship that the audience had with the action in sport and the spontaneous and impulsive responses that were elicited by the action.

Brecht's career was very closely linked to his fellow German theatre director Erwin Piscator. Piscator was most interested in political theatre and the idea of agitation propaganda or 'agit prop' theatre, in which theatre was a vehicle for protest and social change. Piscator was also very interested in the spectacle of theatre and would often use large casts, technically sophisticated staging and projection. Brecht learnt much from Piscator in these terms. However, he wanted to create a simpler storytelling technique, where the audience were challenged into thought and judgment – he did not want them to be overwhelmed by the theatricality or the message.

For a real understanding of how Brecht changed and redefined theatre, we need to realise what had gone on before him in terms of theatre history. Brecht was reacting against the form and content of plays. Stanislavski's system and the advent and consolidation of 'realism' within European theatre had made Brecht determined to change the place of theatre within society. He also wanted to change the attitude of the audience towards plays. German audiences were mainly bourgeois and took theatre very seriously, viewing it as art with their role as passive onlookers. He wanted to make theatre popular, relevant and accessible.

Key concepts

If Stanislavski's work was concerned with empathy, feelings and the heart, then Brecht could be considered as someone concerned with distance, thinking and reason. These basic principles were the foundation for what Brecht called **epic theatre**. Let's break this down into some key areas.

Other theatre forms

Brecht also became aware from Japanese noh theatre that the role of the audience could become much more active rather than passive. Noh plays are often morality stories that require a response or judgement from the audience. This influenced his important notion of alienation.

Sporting events

Erwin Piscator

Brecht later felt much more at ease with the ideas of the designer Caspar Neher, who worked closely with Brecht to create stage pictures with sets and staging that complemented the action and supported the actors.

Theatre before Brecht

Brecht should not necessarily be cast in opposition to Stanislavski – this is perhaps too simplistic, despite their opposing ideas. Brecht was a huge admirer of Stanislavski's work, and much of Brecht's work was only possible as a consequence of the Russian's thoughts and theories.

Further reading

See Brecht's comparison of dramatic and epic theatre in *Brecht on Theatre*, ed John Willett (Methuen 1978).

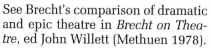

The audience

See pages 15 and 31 for more on the fourth wall.

Alienation

> The theatre-goer in conventional theatre says: Yes, I've felt that way too.... I am made to cry with those who cry, and laugh with those who laugh. But the theatre-goer in the epic theatre says: I would never have thought that.... I am made to laugh about those who cry and cry about those who laugh.

Bertolt Brecht, *On Theatre*, trans. John Willett (Methuen 1964)

The actor

> Whereas Stanislavsky, in Brecht's view, can only offer us artificial reconstructions of reality, Brecht is determined to 'show things as they are'. The premium is still on 'truth' but the definitions have altered.

Shomit Mitter, *Systems of rehearsal: Stanislavsky, Brecht, Grotowski, and Brook* (New York 1992)

Brecht held the work of Charlie Chaplin in great esteem for this reason.

Brecht really wanted to create a new relationship between the play and the audience. He argued that the invisible fourth wall created by Stanislavski made the audience much more passive. They were drawn into the fiction of the drama, but could do nothing to change the situations, characters or the ending. They became emotionally involved with the situations and characters, but did not think about why the situations had occurred and what that might mean.

In order to get the audience more mentally engaged with the play Brecht developed the notion of the **Verfremdungseffekt**, which is now referred to in English as the **alienation effect**. This is not an easy word to translate, and has often been misinterpreted or misunderstood – it is not concerned with literally 'alienating' the audience from the play.

What Brecht was trying to achieve was a set of theatrical devices to make the play seem strange (alien) to the audience, so that they would be forced to think about the events, action and characters in a new and unfamiliar way. Brecht wanted the audience to become more involved, to be both emotionally engaged in a scene and then immediately stand outside it to think about it, and to make a judgment on it. He was not afraid of emotion and understood the power of it in performance, but he wanted his audience to be able to stand back from it at times, to analyse it.

The role of the actor in this process was vital. Whereas Stanislavski required his actors to identify with their roles and embody them on stage, Brecht wanted his actors to distance themselves from the characters they were playing. He created many devices to help his actors achieve this distance. He felt his actors should **demonstrate** rather than become a role. He saw them very much as storytellers, who could play many parts and have a view of the characters they were playing. Within his plays and performances he allowed his actors to multi-role and allowed the audience to see the actor changing parts. He allowed them to step out of their emotional engagement with a character to look critically at what they represented.

An actor might do the following things to ensure they are 'demonstrating' in this way:

➢ Play more than one role and change from role to role in plain view of the audience.

➢ Speak in the third person.

➢ Transpose the dialogue into the past tense.

➢ Speak the stage instructions.

➢ Use very clear, stylised body language, facial expression, tone of voice and movement to reflect the social status and outlook of that character. This is referred to as **Gest** or gestus.

➢ Use costume (or tokens of costume) to help clearly define characters.

➢ Use song to introduce or comment on the action of a scene, so that the audience can step back and be objective, and begin to analyse why certain events happen.

In the period before Brecht, plays were very much concerned with a clear narrative that flowed from one scene to another. Within these stories issues would be raised by characters and their interaction with each other, but resolved by the end. Brecht was also concerned with storytelling and narrative, but he felt this did not necessarily have to be linear in style – the story could begin, stop and travel anywhere. The story itself could also be fragmented and made up of self-contained scenes or episodes. This episodic work was known as **montage**.

Brecht thought that another way to make the audience look strangely at the play would be to break the unities of action, time and place, and fragment the chronology and linear nature of the story. He thus broke his plays down into episodes to show that theatre could be like a piece of expressionist art or a film. By placing together scenes of unequal length, seemingly unrelated and presented in differing styles, he forced the audience to think about their relevance and relationship to the story, the characters and themselves.

The episodes themselves could be in a variety of styles, and could shift modes from a multi-character scene to a monologue or even narration to keep the audience engaged – but also to help them refocus and remain objective.

 Think about how films use editing and montage to continually challenge the audience and get them to re-focus on the ideas of the film. Good examples of recent films which use inventive editing would be *Pulp Fiction* (1994), which breaks the unities of time and action to complicate the plot and reinvent the journeys of the characters, and *Memento* (2000), which tells a story in reverse to force the audience to make judgments on what happened and why.

Brecht was really clear that he wanted the mechanics of theatre shown to his audiences. He did not want them to try to 'suspend their disbelief', but rather always to know that they were in a theatre and watching a fiction. With this in mind, the set could be simple or suggested using staging or props that represented locations. If there was a change in time or location then that could be shown to the audience in the way that the set was changed or moved.

He also thought that placards and projections could swiftly communicate to the audience changes in action, time and place. Lighting was used only to illuminate the action of the story, and was not to be used to create subliminal effects or moods in support of the action. If colours or effects were employed then Brecht insisted that their use was explained to the audience, so that they were not deceived into feeling but were led into thinking.

All these ideas served to emphasise the anti-illusionary approach to theatre, forcing the audience to recognise that they were in a theatre, and that the all-important element was the meaning of the story, not the spectacle.

The play text

Montage

> " Art is not a mirror held up to reality, but a hammer with which to shape it. "
>
> Ascribed to Brecht

The term 'montage' is credited to the Soviet filmmaker Sergey Eisenstein. In his film *Battleship Potemkin* (1925) he used montage to create a powerful series of episodes on the Odessa Steps to show the Tsarist troops brutally quelling a civilian riot. The juxtaposition, contrast and counterpoint of images created a moving and disturbing sequence. This was exactly the effect that Brecht was trying to achieve in theatre.

Staging

Web link

Andrew Moore's teaching resource site at www.universalteacher.org.uk is very clear and helpful in its description of the stages of Brecht's plays and thinking.

Phases of Brecht's thinking

Period	Important works	Commentary
The early period	*Trommeln in der Nacht* (*Drums in the Night*, 1918) *Mann ist Mann* (*Man is Man*, 1924–1925) *Die Dreigroschenoper* (*The Threepenny Opera*, 1928) *Mahagonny* (*The Rise and Fall of the Town of Mahagonny*, 1928–1929)	The plays were humorous in a rather bleak and cynical way, and presented social and political questions attacking bourgeois values.
The learning plays	*Der Flug des Lindberghs* [*Der Ozeanflug*] (*The Flight of Lindbergh* [*the Ocean Flight*]) *Das Badener Lehrstück vom Einverständnis*, (*The Bavarian Parable Play of Understanding*) *Der Jasager* (*The Yes-Sayer*) *Der Neinsager* (*The No-Sayer*) *Die Massnahme* (*The Measures Taken*) *Die Ausnahme und die Regel* (*The Exception and the Rule*)	The *Lehrstücke* (teaching plays) were short, parabolic pieces, written between 1928 and 1930. These plays, which were written to instruct children, were not attractive to audiences. They earned Brecht the reputation of being very **didactic** – trying to use his plays to teach lessons and make points. This led the playwright Ionesco to call him 'the Postman', as he only wanted to deliver messages. *Der Ozeanflug*, broadcast as a radio play, was produced without the reading of the main part, which was to be spoken by the audience, who were supplied with scripts. There were also three longer propaganda plays: *Die Heilige Johanna der Schlachthöfe* (*St Joan of the Stockyards* [slaughterhouses]), which parodied Shakespeare, Schiller and Goethe (and Shaw's *Major Barbara*), and contained many devices of what became epic theatre, such as a loudspeaker announcing political events of the time, or projection of captions commenting on the drama; *Die Mutter* (*The Mother*), which dealt explicitly and didactically with political revolution; and *Die Rundköpfe und die Spitzköpfe* (*The round-heads and the pointy-heads*), a play that took its plot from Shakespeare's *Measure for Measure* but also dealt with the Nazi emphasis on inferior and superior races.
The later years	*Mutter Courage und ihre Kinder* (*Mother Courage and her children*, 1941) *Leben des Galilei* (*Life of Galileo*, 1943) *Der Gute Mensch von Setzuan* (*The Good Person of Setzuan*, 1943) *Der kaukasische Kreidekreis* (*The Caucasian Chalk-Circle*, performed in English in 1947; in German not until 1954)	The first two of these plays contained episodic narrative theatre – each scene prefaced by a caption indicating what happened. In the third play the scenes presenting the action were followed by interludes, in which the actors stood back from their roles and commented on the actions of their characters. In *The Caucasian Chalk-Circle*, Brecht used a play within the play: in order to resolve the conflict of two groups of peasants who wished to farm a valley, a play is presented by the singer, musicians and actors. The singer and musicians stood outside the drama of Grusche, Azdak, Simon and Natella, and provided both narrative and commentary. These plays are very much a part of the **dialectic** style – whereby Brecht wanted to use scenes and situations to create an argument with all sides shown, and with the audience incited to play an active role in making their own mind up during the play, and when they leave the theatre.

Brecht in practice

In order to understand Brecht's concepts fully you need to try to apply them practically. Rather than give you small exercises to work on each concept, as with the Stanislavski material above, here you will find a large three-step approach to practical work that tests your understanding of Brecht's epic theatre as a whole.

 ### Stage one – the accident

There has been a road accident, and as a passerby you have been a spectator to it.

Imagine you are telling the story to a group of people who did not see the accident. Tell the story and include all the characters that were in it. Feel free to impersonate or even caricature them. Try to use gest, narration, dialogue, third person, descriptions and even token costume to bring the story to life.

This exercise allows the actor to demonstrate the characters within the story and use devices to make the story fresh and strange to the audience. It also supports the anti-illusionary aspect of theatre, in that the audience is aware that the passer-by is just telling the story and is not really any of the characters within it. However, it also gives the audience an insight into the attitude and judgement of the storyteller.

Choose someone else who was involved in the accident and completely retell the story from their point of view. If you are working in a group then agree the facts of the accident, and then each of you work out your version of events. Show these versions to each other to see how different they can be from varying perspectives.

 ### Stage two – a well-known story

This is an excellent exercise to try in a small group. Remember that Brecht wanted theatre to be fun and exciting, like spectator sport. See if you can have fun with this by doing it at pace and with real wit.

Choose a story that all of your group knows. A good example would be *The Three Little Pigs*.

Decide what set, staging items or props you will use in advance. You may use a table to represent the houses in the story. You may choose to use no props at all but create and indicate the locations with members of your group forming shapes.

1. **The story:** Improvise the story using dialogue and action only, with each member of your group playing a different character.

2. **The narrator:** You must now build on your initial improvisation by adding narration. Each of your group must add a narrative speech to introduce their characters and describe some element of the action.

3. **The monologue:** Give each of your characters an opportunity to present their thoughts and views with a short monologue.

4. **The attitude:** You must now build on step three by allowing each of your characters an opportunity to speak in the third person, to indicate the attitudes and feeling of the character they are beginning to demonstrate. You could perhaps introduce and/or close their monologue with this.

5. **The placard:** Create a number of placards with pens and card that do a number of things. Use some placards to introduce location, time and/or character. Use other placards to indicate the attitude and internal thoughts of the characters

6. **The gest:** Choose a moment, a scene or even a character and create a movement/body language sequence that demonstrates who they are and how they are feeling. This can be as simple as the wolf arriving at each of the houses with the expectation of a meal.

7. **The music:** Choose a song or a piece of music that you think could introduce or comment on some action of the play. Be as topical as you want – choose a piece of current music from the charts or a film, or use something more traditional. Think about what you want the music to say when it is juxtaposed against a particular scene or moment.

8. **Shifting modes:** You must now build on step seven by rearranging the chronology and structure of the story. You must create a series of episodes that are no longer in chronological order. You could perhaps begin with the ending. The episodes must also shift between different modes of presentation, such as scenes of monologue, extended narration, dialogue, action, song and gest. Try to surprise your audience.

9. **Alienation:** Perform your piece, and discuss whether you have found a way of making the story strange and fresh to an audience. If so, in what way?

 ## Stage three – a news story

This can be quite a disturbing exercise but it really helps you get to grips with the *Verfremdungseffekt*. You could work by yourself or in a group on this exercise.

Take a recent news story that deals with a serious crime. If it is a well-documented crime, such as the Yorkshire Moors murders, then there will be lots of material available through Internet sites. If you feel uncomfortable with exploring a recent crime then you could perhaps look at a more historical or fictitious crime such as Jack the Ripper or Sweeney Todd. The objective of this exercise is to retell the story, making it strange to the audience so that they can view the crime with a fresh perspective.

After a period of research, your task is straightforward. Create a piece of epic theatre that uses montage and episodic scenes to retell the story of a serious crime. Use the steps from Stage 2 to help you approach the task. Try to make the piece dialectic and not didactic. Try not to suggest or impose answers and judgements, but set out problems and questions for the audience to think about and decide upon.

See the table on phases of Brecht's thinking (page 22) for more on dialectic and didactic.

Further reading

The following concepts can be explored in more detail in the collection of Artaud's essays *The Theatre and its Double* (Calder 1998) and *Antonin Artaud: Blows and Bombs* by Stephen Barber (Faber and Faber 1994).

Rehearsing theatre: Artaud

The theatrical legacy of Antonin Artaud (1896–1948) is not a structured series of exercises or a method for actors to follow. Instead, Artaud's work provides a vision that stems from his violent hatred of realism. He represents the other end of the performance scale from Stanislavski: he wanted not to portray realism in his productions but to transcend it – a theatre that challenged the audience, forcing them to see new ideas and values. His ideas may initially appear fragmented and at times incoherent, but through his writings, sketches, recordings and photographs one is able to create a sense of a man whose passion for change was coupled with extreme frustration and mental torture.

Life and background

Artaud was born in Marseilles into a strict religious family which he found suffocating. He had a troubled childhood, suffering from meningitis and depression, the symptoms of which led to him being isolated at school. He was extremely strong-willed and reluctant to conform to the conventions of society: as a consequence of this, his parents arranged for him to be incarcerated in a sanatorium in 1915, where he remained for a period of five years. During this time, he was prescribed opium and this was the start of a long-standing addiction to drugs.

Once released, Artaud embarked on a fascinating series of experiences that helped him to formulate his extreme views on both society and theatre. He was a prolific poet and became extremely angry when his work was rejected by the magazine *La Nouvelle Revue Française*. In 1924, he became an active and influential member of the surrealist movement. He and the surrealists shared a political viewpoint based around anarchy and free-thinking, and a vision of the theatre as a place not for bourgeois entertainment but for emotional discovery. However, the relationship between Artaud and the group was often strained and two years later he was expelled. He acted in many films and was celebrated for his non-realist style.

In 1931, Artaud witnessed a performance by Balinese dancers in Paris that acted as a catalyst for the development of his theatre. Balinese dance-drama is religious in nature and involves the acting out of Hindu legends in a stylised way, with the use of deeply unrealistic make-up, symbolic masks and hand-gestures. The performances are given in local tongues, accompanied by percussion.

Artaud was struck by the magical quality of the work. The dancers' dependence on gestures, facial expressions and visuals created a physical language that appealed to the unconscious. The focus was not on the distant words of a playwright but on the direct relationship between director, actor and audience. Artaud was impressed by the fact that his experience of the performance was (since he understood no Balinese) independent of a verbal language. This, he argued, was the true purpose of theatre: to offer something that could not be offered by a novel or poem, or any other medium. Without language or a familiarity with the story, drama is more effective, more visceral, more engaging. He wanted to devise drama that appeared to his audiences as the Balinese dance-drama appeared to him.

Two other influences affected the development of his ideas. The first was the painting *The Daughters of Lot* by Leyden, which he saw at the Louvre. He frequently took friends to see it and monitored their response. The violent images in the painting had a theatrical quality to them and he considered the impact that such a still image could have on stage. The second influence was film and in particular the work of the Marx Brothers. Artaud was fascinated

Web link

See the site www.hydra.umn.edu/ artaud for excerpts from Artaud's writings, etchings and further web links.

Surrealism

" What separates me from the surrealists is that they love life as much as I despise it. "

Artaud, *Point final* (Paris 1927)

Balinese dance-drama

" Dialogue does not specifically belong to the stage but to books. I maintain the stage is a tangible, physical place that needs to be filled, and it ought to be allowed to speak its own concrete language. "

Artaud, 'Production and metaphysics' in *The Theatre and its Double*, trans. Victor Corti (Calder 1998)

Other influences

by the manner in which they juxtaposed images to create humour. Their non-realist style was liberating and he quickly realised the potential power of laughter within his theatre.

Theatre of Cruelty

Artaud organised his ideas into a manifesto, called the Theatre of Cruelty. He used the word cruelty in the broadest sense, implying that theatre should go to the very extreme of all that a director can exert on the actor and the spectator. His aim was to reinvent the theatrical experience, abolishing the traditions of realism, and allowing design and performance skills to work together to maximise the sensory experience of the audience.

Before we can experiment with practical ideas it is important to understand the essence of Artaud's theatre. It was revolutionary, which partly explains why he was unable to achieve a production that did justice to all of his aims.

The auditorium

His desire to break from the restrictions of psychological theatre started with the nature of the performance space. The stage building should be a single, undivided locale, probably a barn or a hanger, which would allow direct communication between the actors and audience. All decoration needed to be removed from the space so that every area could be used. The audience would be in the middle on swivel chairs, while a walkway would be built around the edges of the auditorium to enable certain action to take place above the spectators. The show, as Artaud called his performance, would fill the space, using different areas and levels to engulf the audience and assault their senses.

Sound

Artaud believed that traditional theatre was a slave to dialogue, so he tried to redefine the aural experience. He believed language prevented the actor from fulfilling their vocal potential, and instead focused on sounds rather than words. Screams were extremely important to him since they represented the most primitive emotion.

> "In Europe, nobody knows how to scream anymore."
>
> Artaud, *The Theatre and its Double*, trans. Victor Corti (Calder 1998)

He considered musical instruments to be very important, both through their ritualistic associations and their ability to create mood and atmosphere. He demanded experimentation in order to generate a new scale in the octave that could vibrate through the body, and oversized instruments that could become a visual part of the performance. The notes would be accompanied by recorded sounds of church bells or footsteps, which could be played at a high volume.

Costume and design

All costume should be devoid of any contemporary relevance and should be specifically designed for each show. However, he felt it might be appropriate to look at images from the past and designs that might take their influences from certain cultural rituals. Artaud believed that the performance could be enriched by traditional outfits which have a certain mystical beauty. Masks and even puppets were encouraged as a way of moving away from realism and discovering a new physical expression that added a dream-like quality to the performance.

Lighting

As Artaud was forming his ideas, technical equipment was limited. Although he was able to isolate key areas of the stage or flood the performance space with light, he envisaged that more sophisticated equipment was necessary in order to release the power of his show. He demanded the discovery of oscillating light effects, new ways of diffusing light in waves, sheet lighting 'like a flight of arrows'. Colour was to be used with subtlety and finesse in order to communicate complex images. Recent advances in lighting technology such as lasers, strobes and computer-controlled effects are excellent examples of Artaud's vision.

Using the principles of Artaud's theatre, create a design for a performance of *Oedipus Rex* by Sophocles. (If you are unfamiliar with the play, look at the plot outline on page 48.) Sit the audience in the centre and consider how each of the elements above could be used to increase the impact of a production.

Other important concepts

The plague

When formulating his ideas, Artaud struggled to find a notion that could encapsulate everything he was thinking and imagining. He settled on the metaphor of the plague and became so inspired by it that he made it the opening chapter of his collected writings. He considered how the plague attacked the lungs and the brain of the body but also affected the heart of society. It had the ability to disrupt order, to release individuals from social conventions and drive them to extremes. This was how his theatre would affect his audience; they would be shaken and irritated by the inner dynamism of the spectacle. After the performance, however, the audience would be purified. He concludes his essay with a passionate declaration of his theatre's power:

> Theatre action is as beneficial as the plague, impelling us to see ourselves as we are, making the masks fall and divulging our world's lies, aimlessness, meanness and even two-facedness. It shakes off stifling material dullness which even overcomes the senses' clearest testimony, and collectively reveals their dark powers and hidden strength to men, urging them to take a nobler, more heroic stand in the face of destiny.
>
> Artaud, *The Theatre and its Double*, trans. Victor Corti
> (Calder 1998)

Ritual

Artaud's writings are filled with references to the religions of different cultures. He was clearly fascinated by their mystical quality and their ability to generate a heightened level of engagement from those who participated. This concept was essential if Artaud's theatre was going to bring about change in his audience.

The easiest way of understanding the idea is thinking in terms of personal experience. What rituals do you participate in? A religious service clearly serves as an excellent example if you feel emotionally engaged with the ceremony, but it is possible to consider ritual in a broader sense. For example, your routine of getting ready in the morning may be so well structured that at the end of the process you feel your mental state has changed. This process of change is central to understanding the power of ritual.

Artaud proposed the use of rhythms, chants, choral speaking and choreographed movement as a way of emulating the experience of more formal ceremonies.

The double

Artaud, through his associations with the surrealist movement, became fascinated by the concepts of both dream and reality working together to produce a heightened reality or 'surreality'. Realistic theatre was preoccupied with mirroring life on stage, but Artaud felt it was unable to show the darker thoughts that can sometimes fill our minds. Imagine how much more intense your experience of the world would be if you knew the dreams of everyone you met. Their unconscious thoughts would no longer be suppressed and would have to be confronted.

The 'double' idea was linked to the concept of the **doppleganger**, most easily identified in the story of Jekyll and Hyde, in which Hyde represents the hidden side of Jekyll's character. Presenting both of these characters on stage would undermine any tendency to revert back to realistic acting.

 Improvise a scene in which a teacher is lecturing a pupil about their behaviour. The pupil is outwardly polite and apologetic. Now repeat the scene, introducing a third character, the doppleganger of the student, who should physically and vocally express their frustration.

Artaud and The Cenci

Unlike Stanislavski and Brecht, Artaud never managed to achieve a successful production. Much of his life was spent exploring and reacting to different stimuli and consequently his ideas lack order and have a limited practical awareness. However, he did manage to produce one of his scenarios called *The Cenci*, which was based on Shelley's tragedy and a document by the French author Stendhal.

The plot is extremely violent and contains images of rape, torture and murder. The protagonist Cenci (the role Artaud played) is eventually killed by his two servants when they plunge nails into his throat and one of his eyes. The graphic and disturbing nature of the stimulus was important to Artaud. He believed that such images had the power to release the audience from their current mental state and make them confront their dreams and primitive instincts. This journey would have a cathartic quality, liberating and cleansing the spectator.

Unfortunately, his show was full of compromise. It was performed in the round, breaking the theatrical convention of the time and did contain some of the images and sound collages he had strived to achieve. However, it was heavily reliant on text and fell short of many of his ideals. After 17 performances and a series of damning reviews, the production closed.

One of Artaud's difficulties was trying to make his cast understand his vision. His constant references to different literary works left them confused. He became quickly frustrated and exhausted by the whole experience.

> "A real stage play upsets our tranquillity, releases our repressed sub-conscious, drives us to a kind of rebellion."
>
> Artaud, *The Theatre and its Double*, trans. Victor Corti (Calder 1998)

Artaud believed that each scenario should only be performed once: 'Let's recognise that what has been said does not need to be said again; that an expression is worth nothing second time, and does not live twice.' Artaud, *Collected Works*, ed. Paul Thevenin (Gallimard 1976).

Exploring Artaud

In order to understand Artaud's philosophy, it is important to try to realise his ideas practically. To attempt simply to intellectualise his Theatre of Cruelty is to misunderstand its power. Some of the ideas for experimentation presented here will appear strange and perhaps embarrassing, but by committing to the exercise you will gain an overview of his approach.

Get into groups of six. Number each other 1 to 6. Number 1 begins by creating an image in the space. Freeze. 2 enters and forms another image that must react to 1's position in some way while making contact with them. 3 enters and forms another freeze, making sure they touch one of the people on stage. Repeat the process until all six actors are on stage. 1 should now move from their initial position and form a new image in reaction to the other five while keeping physical contact with someone. Repeat the process with all the other numbers and allow the shape to evolve continually.

Ask a group of people to watch the exercise and give feedback on moments they thought were of interest. You will probably experience two different responses. Some will impose characters onto the scene and attempt to find a narrative order to the work. For example, they may identify a victim who is bullied or a group who are travelling on a journey. Others will perceive it from an emotional perspective so that they associate with the fear or anger (or whatever emotion) at a given moment. The latter is closer to Artaud's vision, in which images communicated directly with the audience's unconscious.

In his essay 'An Affective Athleticism', Artaud stressed the importance of physical training for the actor. Not only should the actor learn to understand the body but also harness its power in order to achieve maximum impact. In society, it is smothered by rules, unable to express itself properly. In the Theatre of Cruelty, it would be released.

Clear parallels can be drawn between his theatrical aims and his personal experiences of mental institutions. He was often held in a straight jacket, restricting his physical freedom, and despite constantly battling with an addiction to drugs, he feared moments in sleep or drunkenness when he was out of control.

His main focus was on breathing and its relationship with the state of the soul. In a concept similar to Stanislavski's emotion memory, he advocates a precise command of breathing, since he believed it was inversely proportional to external expression. The more restrained the emotion, the more intense the breathing becomes. However, in moments of extreme anger, breath is used in short controlled bursts.

Experiment with improvising two scenes looking at these two contrasting states. First, imagine a scene between an employer and employee in which the latter is publicly and viciously embarrassed and then sacked in front of their colleagues. Initially, experiment with the worker as unable to talk, focusing on the intensity of the breathing. Make each breath audible and

Practical experimentation

> " I am well aware that a language of gestures and postures, dance and music is less able to define a character. But whoever said theatre was made to define a character? "
>
> Artaud, *The Theatre and its Double*, trans. Victor Corti (Calder 1998)

Artaud and the body

This essay is in *The Theatre and its Double*. Note the difference between 'affective' and 'effective': affective refers to the production or arousal of emotions.

intense. Repeat the scene with the employee now able to answer back. Use bursts of dialogue and breath control.

Just as an athlete uses certain muscle groups to increase performance, Artaud felt his actors should become familiar with certain localised points as a way of exploring emotion. Many of his ideas stemmed from the Chinese concept of acupuncture. He believed fright and sorrow originated in the small of the back, anger and attack came from the solar plexus and heroism derived from the chest. By focusing on these areas and moving between them, shades of emotion could be explored in their truest form.

The solar plexus is between the chest and the navel.

The body was the foundation for the Theatre of Cruelty and the regular rhythm of the heart, the power of breath control and the immediacy of the scream became essential tools in achieving his goals.

It may be useful to try this exercise in pairs with one person reading the instructions while the other follows. Lie on your back, put your hands by your side and bend your knees so the soles of your feet are flat on the floor. Breathe in through your nose and out through your mouth. Monitor your breathing and try to slow it down. Every time you exhale, turn the breath into a hum. Try to maintain it for as long as possible. Continue to do this while focusing on your body. How do your feet feel? Are they comfortable, tired, tense? Work your way up through your body. Focus on your stomach. Is it full? Bloated? Is it hungry? Instead of humming, try to express how your stomach feels through abstract noise. Now focus on the heart. Is it fit and healthy? Does it feel like blood is flowing freely or is it a real effort to send it through the body? Vocalise this feeling. Using the rhythm of your heart, convert this feeling into a combination of vocal and physical work.

If several people have tried this exercise, ask them all to perform at the same time, so that you have a collage of hearts. This all may appear strange on the page or even embarrassing to perform but the key is the potential impact it has on an audience.

Acting Artaud

Artaud's theatre relied on a form of spatial expression. It focused on image rather than language and the combination of actor and design skills helped to ensure a total theatrical experience. We have already looked at his theatre as being against the traditions of psychological realism, but ironically realism is a useful tool in accessing some of Artaud's ideas.

Consider a scene in which an actor is smoking a cigarette. Stanislavski might ask an actor to focus on their motivation for smoking, how the cigarette is held, what this might reveal about the character. Artaud would begin by focusing on the body and in particular the lungs as the smoke is inhaled, the gathering of tar and the emotional kick of the nicotine. Rather than simply using this as an internal reference for the actor he might encourage the actor to express this sensation externally through a series of physical gestures and abstract sounds which have no link to the reality of the action. He saw this being true to the essence of the act, rather than asking an audience to read the impact of such an event on the face of a character.

" Actors should be like torture victims who are being burned and making signs from the stake. "
Artaud, *Collected Works*, ed. Paul Thevenin (Gallimard 1976)

Experiment with the following ideas, moving from realistic to more symbolic acting. Although the exercises are suitable for pairs, it is often useful to try the activity at the same time as others, which will allow you to experience a variety of interpretations and look at the impact of performing several images at the same time.

Consider the story of Oedipus and his wife Jocasta. Unbeknown to them both, Jocasta is also Oedipus' mother. When she discovers the truth, Jocasta goes to her room and hangs herself. When Oedipus discovers her, he removes two brooches from her dress and stabs out his eyes. Try performing this in a semi realistic style, miming the hanging and blinding. Repeat the exercise to a count of 20, 10 for Jocasta's actions, 10 for Oedipus'. Now consider how an Artaudian actor might perform the section. At this stage no words are permitted, neither can there be a realistic mime of hanging or stabbing of eyes. The focus should be on the internal feeling and how it might be expressed externally. It doesn't matter if people watching aren't able to identify what you are doing. Remember, Artaud's theatre is not driven by character. Perform the entrance of Jocasta and Oedipus over a count of 20. Experiment with other pairs performing their scenes at the same time as yours. What is the impact of such work? Does Artaud's style dilute or concentrate the experience?

In Sophocles' *Oedipus Rex*, this all takes place offstage and is reported in a vivid messenger speech.

Try the nursery rhyme *Little Miss Muffet*. Consider it first from a Stanislavskian perspective. Why did Miss Muffet sit on her tuffet? Was it a calm act on a summer's day or a moment of defiance from a young girl who had been sent to her room? Why did the spider approach her? Was he trying to intimidate, was he lonely or did he have a liking for curds and whey?

Perform the scene in a realistic style. Repeat to a count of 20, exaggerating the characterisation by emphasising the emotion. Now repeat the exercise in the style of Artaud. Focus on the emotions experienced in the scene and express these physically through physical tension and abstract sound. This second version is clearly more comical but remember humour was considered to be a powerful force and it is important that you experiment with it in different forms.

There is no doubt that a true Artaudian performance would be an assault on the senses of any spectator. The staging itself was designed to make them feel trapped and before his performance of *The Cenci* Artaud indicated his desire for his audience to be plunged into a bath of fire participating with their souls and nerves. Although he was never able to achieve this onslaught, it is easy to imagine how his performance style could be threatening.

The concept of swivelling seats adds an interesting dynamic, undermining the more formal rows of the traditional proscenium-arch theatres. It allows the audience to participate actively, choosing where to look and when to turn. His staging removed the reliance on the imaginary fourth wall between actor and audience. This barrier would have prevented the direct communication that Artaud felt was necessary in engaging the inner sense of all who experienced his show.

In order to understand the power of his theatre fully, one has to experience it from an audience's perspective. During the next few exercises it is important that you experiment with both performing and watching the work. By understanding how it feels to be

Involving an audience

surrounded by performers, you will gain a greater insight into the potential power of the performance.

Get into a group of at least five people, one of whom will need to leave the room while the performance is prepared. When they re-enter, they will be blindfolded and will experience the work through their other senses. Find a photograph in a newspaper or magazine of a scene from life that creates a specific mood or emotion. For example, consider the image of a slightly jaded-looking cottage with an old person asleep in a worn armchair. Discuss the feel of the scene and how you might convey that through sound, touch and movement. You can use realistic sound effects like the breathing of the old person, but also experiment with conveying the atmosphere of the scene. Try to organise your ideas into an order and rehearse the scene. When you are ready, invite the volunteer back into the room and actively involve them in your environment as you perform the work. Lead them around the space and encourage them to explore key areas through touch.

Once the exercise is complete, ask the volunteer to feed back what they understood by the experience. The level of response will vary tremendously and could range from phrases like 'I could sense death in the room' to 'there was a coal fire in the corner'. Repeat the exercise with different images and volunteers to see if the group can hone their technique.

Get into groups of four or five. Choose a nursery rhyme and try to recreate it in the style of Artaud. Remember your audience will be sat in the middle. Don't feel limited by character – experiment with how choreographed sound and synchronised movement could be used to convey the scene. Avoid using traditional speech. Try switching the action from one end of the room to the other and invading the audience space in the middle.

After the piece has been rehearsed, perform it to an audience. How did they react? Were they able to identify the nursery rhyme? Did this affect their experience? How did sitting in the centre intensify the experience?

> " The overlapping of images and movements will, by the conspiracies of objects, of silences, of cries and of rhythms, arrive at the creation of a true physical language based on signs and not words. "
>
> Artaud, *Collected Works*, ed. Paul Thevenin (Gallimard 1976)

It could be argued that dipping into Artaud's ideas and using them to reinvent the theatre form is a betrayal of his vision. However, as actors, you will need to experiment with a range of styles that not only demonstrate a knowledge and understanding of other practitioners, but also a command of different techniques which will enable you to communicate your ideas successfully. Experimentation is the key to success. Be brave in your approach and select those ideas which best suit your needs.

Designing theatre

Staging

Every theatrical practitioner has a preferred style of performance. Some will enjoy the intimacy of small studio theatres, others will be excited by grand theatres that allow for spectacular effects. The nature of the staging will ultimately influence the style of acting and the demands placed on set, costume, lighting and sound.

The first theatres in ancient Greece were semi-circular in nature and often cut into a hillside. Thousands of people watched on the curved raised seats looking down on the central performance area. However, it wasn't until the Elizabethan period that the first theatres were built in this country. Although they did utilise some of the Greek traditions, the characteristic Elizabethan stage was the **thrust stage**, which brought the actors out into the audience. This was an important element of the performance style and ensured a direct relationship between the cast and the public.

Thrust stage

'Elizabethan' refers to the reign of Elizabeth I, 1558–1603.

Web link

The Globe Theatre in London is a faithful recreation of such a theatre. Visit www.shakespeare-globe.org

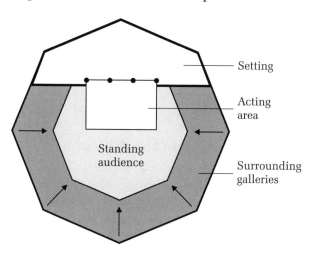

An Elizabethan public theatre

This structure has been reinterpreted over time and has taken on many different guises, particularly in modern theatres. The Swan Theatre in Stratford is a different example of the same style, although you may be more familiar with the structure outlined below:

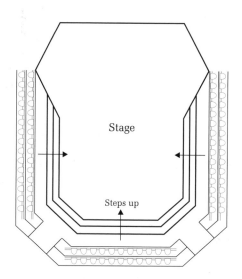

A thrust stage

During this period, private performances of plays were often commissioned by the rich to take place in existing venues such as great halls. These were on a smaller scale and involved an audience sitting in rows, all facing one direction. This became known as **end-on staging**, since all of the action took place at one end of the room.

As the popularity of such performances increased, specially designed theatres were built in order to accommodate the demand. The size of the auditorium meant that the performance space needed to be more clearly defined, so the stage was framed with

End-on and proscenium arch

what has since become known as a **proscenium arch**, which added a certain formality to the performance.

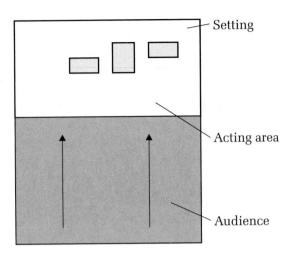

An end-on stage

The increasingly complex and detailed nature of the staging meant that playwrights wrote longer, more detailed scenes (for fewer scene changes), and new techniques were developed in order to create different locations in the large performance area. This became the predominant performance style, although by the turn of the 20th century certain practitioners had become frustrated with the formality of this method of staging.

Theatre in the round

See pages 24–32 for more on Artaud and his concept of theatre.

In a reaction against realism, Antonin Artaud wanted his audience to be trapped in the middle of the auditorium, with the actors performing around them. A more popular concept that has evolved is the exact reversal of this: the audience are positioned on all four sides of the performance space, surrounding the actors. This is usually termed **theatre in the round**. It can be difficult to direct, as the actors will invariably always block the view of some of the audience and set has to be kept to a minimum. Having said this, it is an extremely intimate experience, which enables the audience to remain focused on the action while being aware of the reaction of other audience members. Street theatre often works on this principle, since the performer has to define their space in a public area.

The Round at the Stephen Joseph Theatre in Scarborough is an example of a theatre that thrives because of this performance style.

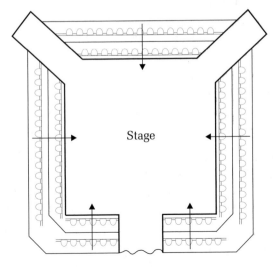

A theatre in the round

While theatre in the round is a fascinating experience, the very nature of the audience's position means that it can often be limiting in terms of design. A traverse stage has the audience on two sides facing each other while allowing for two clear areas at either end for fixed set or group images. The audience can at times feel they are watching a tennis match as their heads follow the action back and forth across the space. The style is particularly suited for comedy, as it enables members of the audience to feed off the reactions of one another.

Traverse staging

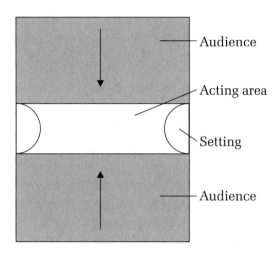

A traverse stage

A promenade performance can be one of the most exciting staging methods, and although it is often used in modern productions, it links back to some of the most early drama work. The concept is extremely simple. The audience is encouraged to walk around the venue following the action. The performance could be located in the ruins of an old church or in a large hall or barn. Their movement is led by the stage action and there is a certain amount of skill thus needed to control the audience's focus. The style does allow for elements of surprise however, since characters or pieces of set can be introduced behind them while their focus is held elsewhere.

Promenade performance

Set design

The nature of the set is clearly influenced by the audience position and the style of the piece. Certain performances may require an accurate recreation of a room in a certain period. Other plays may allow total freedom for the designer, where the only limit is their own imagination. If you have little experience of design then it is important that you start by visualising key images. This may be based on one of the locations implied in the script or it could stem from the mood of the piece. Try to sketch these ideas on paper and then use the starting-points below to create your design formally.

- ➤ **Size**: What are the dimensions of your performance space (width, depth and height)? Draw an outline of the stage to scale on your set plan. Will **tabs** (curtains) or **flats** (wooden scenery) be used to frame the space? Is there a need for a painted backdrop?

- ➤ **Scale**: Will your design fill the stage space? Will it be in proportion with the actors using it? For example, a large sweeping staircase or a small crooked door may reflect some of the themes of the play.

Web link

An impressive directory of set, lighting, costume and sound can be found at http://dmoz.org/Arts/Performing_Arts/Theatre/Stagecraft. There are many examples which will help both new and experienced designers.

> **Period**: Will your set need to transport your audience to a different moment in time, past or future? If the play is set in the present, which aspects of the modern world does it reflect?

> **Colour**: How could you use colour to create an appropriate atmosphere? Black and white can symbolise a cold environment, whereas bold colours on a table might emphasise its significance.

> **Texture**: Should the floor of the stage be rough or smooth? Will the audience have to cross the performance space to get to their seats? What might the texture of the set say about the location or even the world of the play?

> **Entrances and exits**: How do characters enter and leave the space? Does one exit have more significance than another? Are levels used to distance these moments from the main action?

Costume

The nature of your costume will rely heavily on your performance style. Costumes true to the original period of the piece will need to be well-researched, looking in particular at the hemlines and waistlines for women, although these may need to be adapted depending on the physical demands of the performance. It is important to recognise the social context of the play since a character's class may restrict what an actor can wear.

> **Style and genre**: The grandness of design might be a very important aspect of your piece. Certain plays contain set pieces which rely on the impact of the costume. Hats and handbags may become bold reflections of characters. Conversely, your piece may be quite physical with neutral costumes supported by simple signers e.g. a briefcase symbolising a businessman.

> **Themes**: How will the issues explored in the play be represented in the manner in which the characters are dressed? Tightly buttoned jackets may represent the formality of the piece, although if they are slightly ill-fitting it may imply that a character is uncomfortable with this element of society. More abstract pieces may require you to make fantastical designs which represent animals, emotions or even states of mind.

> **Colour**: Consider how colour can reflect both the mood and the status of the character. Hair and make-up could be used to accentuate any personality traits.

Lighting

Some students become intimidated by lighting since it can be the subtlest of all design elements. In a realistic performance, for example, you may be totally unaware of any lighting changes, with the exception of blackouts. Having said this, if it is used creatively it can be an incredibly powerful tool, manipulating audience response without them realising it.

Lanterns   Essentially, there are three main types of lantern: a **profile** (sometimes known as a spotlight), a **fresnel** and a **flood**. They each have slightly different uses and are categorised based on the number of lenses used to control the light output, which is two, one and none respectively. A profile is a sharp, narrow beam of light, whereas a flood produces wide, unfocused light. A fresnel uses a special type of lens to create a spotlight effect.

When designing a lighting rig, you should consider the following:

➢ **Colour**: Coloured gels are used to create different moods, with a straw-like colour frequently used for a warm environment and steel blue used for a cold atmosphere. Lights shone on a white cyclorama will change its colour and ultimately manipulate the mood of the scene. Lanterns without gels create a harsh white light.

➢ **Position**: In a realistic performance, areas of the stage will be lit by a group of lanterns that cancel out any shadows and create a general cover of light, but certain moments within your play may require particular effects. Floor lights at the front of the stage will cast long shadows behind the actors. Lighting directly from above will isolate an actor, often making them look vulnerable. Using a torch held in different positions will help you to discover the best location for your lantern.

➢ **Intensity and fade times**: Once the rig is complete, you will need to consider which lanterns you want on, how bright you want them and the speed of the changes between each of these states.

➢ **Gobos**: These are metal discs that are placed inside profile lanterns to cast a shadow that represents an image. Realistic images like window frames are often used, and rotating gobos can be used to create a swirling hypnotic effect.

Sound

There are very few technical terms to grasp when discussing sound. The skill is mainly in selecting the appropriate effects for the piece. Essentially, your sound will be created either offstage or on stage, or it will be pre-recorded. It could involve a live band, microphones to amplify and distort sounds, or a specific noise that creates an image in the audience's mind. The BBC produces a comprehensive range of sound effects on CD that are readily available, and there is a vast range of effects to download from the Internet.

When designing your play, consider how music – live or recorded – can manipulate mood. Audiences are used to this technique in both television and cinema, and there are many soundtracks to films that would create an extremely powerful opening to certain plays. Sound may be the first design element experienced by an audience, so think carefully about the position of speakers, the volume of each track and the style of music or effect used.

Defining theatre

In addition to the areas of theatre you will explore in significant detail, you are required to be familiar with specific dramatic terminology, some of which is listed below, and some of which can be found in the sections above and in other chapters of this book. Take time to understand each of these concepts, as you need to be able to identify them in the performances you see and produce, and to be able to use the correct names for them when producing your written work.

Further study

Find out about parcan, birdie and strobe lanterns, and how gauze can be used to create lighting effects.

A cyclorama is a large backdrop, usually white, which helps to frame the stage. It is frequently used to represent the sky.

Web link

www.theatrecrafts.com is an excellent website which includes an extensive glossary of theatre terms and practical advice for all elements of theatre design.

Aside　A theatrical convention used for revealing a character's thoughts without the other characters hearing. The structures of Elizabethan theatres lent themselves to such a technique. The actor would move downstage or turn to one area of the audience to provide them with additional information. In tragedies, asides can be used to emphasise the darker thoughts of a character's mind. For example, in Shakespeare's *Macbeth*, Macbeth's amazement as the witches' prophecies come true is revealed through this technique. In comedy, it often highlights the stupidity of the other characters, as the audience are actively encouraged to laugh at their behaviour.

Climax/anti-climax　A climax is a high point in tension usually towards the end of the play where the different strands of the plot all meet. An anti-climax can sometimes follow a climax, particularly when the play has a weak ending. It often leaves the audience feeling disappointed, undermining the excitement created in the previous scene.

Commedia dell'arte　An Italian form of theatre using half-masks, stock characters and stylised movement. Originating in the 16th century, performances took place in public piazzas using simple staging. The action was improvised around a basic plot outline that often included references to sex and greed using a series of rehearsed 'lazzi' or comic scenes. The style has influenced many writers and is most popularly recognisable in the physical work of the Marx brothers and the plays of Dario Fo.

For more on stock characters, see page 9.

Epilogue　The opposite of prologue (see *below*), an epilogue, in dramatic terms, is a formal speech given by one of the characters at the end of the play. Usually written in verse and spoken directly to the audience, it contains the play's message.

Melodrama　The dominant theatrical form of the 19th century. During this period, towns and cities were becoming more industrialised and therefore expanding rapidly. The plays provided entertainment for the masses while allowing a momentary escape from the monotonous and depressing aspects of their lives. The large size of the audience dictated the performance style. Large gestures, exaggerated emotions and stereotyped characters dominated the formulaic plots which saw good conquering evil and the poor outwitting the wealthy. During the latter half of the century, the structure became more sophisticated with greater emphasis being placed on real social dilemmas.

Narrative/narration　Narrative is essentially another word for story: it is the progressive sequence of events or experiences. Narration is the process by which this story or sequence is recited to the audience. Just as poems do not necessarily need to rhyme, plays do not have to have a clear narrative running through them: they may be deliberately fragmented, or have no obvious story at all.

Pantomime A style derived from commedia dell'arte performances by French actors in London during the early 18th century. The stock characters and slapstick comedy evolved and new traditions were established: the 'dame' characters were played by men, the 'principal boy' by a woman. Traditional stories evolved from folk tales. During Victorian times key characters such as Buttons and Widow Twanky were created, the traditional performance time of Christmas was established, and children became the target audience.

Prologue In dramatic terms, serves as an introduction to the play. It is derived from Greek theatre, in which 'the gods' often spoke to the audience before the main action of the play began. Frequently used in Elizabethan (*Romeo and Juliet* is a good example) and Restoration theatre, this device is rarely used in modern dramas. See also **epilogue**.

'Restoration' refers to the reign of Charles II, who was restored to the throne in 1660.

Rhythm A generic theatre term often associated with dance, music or movement. More specifically, certain directors put great emphasis on finding and adopting the rhythm of a character as a rehearsal technique. This can refer to the speed of the walk and the nature of key gestures and emotions. In terms of prose, it's worth noting the ease with which a rhythmic line can be projected by an actor.

For more on this, see the section on tempo-rhythm on page 16.

Projecting the words of Shakespeare and his contemporaries in a bustling Elizabethan theatre was made much easier by the balance and pulse of the **iambic pentameter** (five stressed syllables, often alternating with five unstressed ones) verse form.

Stage directions In the proscenium-arch staging of the 18th century, the stage was often **raked** – raised at the back so that everyone could see what was occurring on stage. As a result, the back of the stage is still called **upstage** and the front **downstage**. The terms **stage right** and **stage left** refer to the actor's right and left as they face the audience (not right and left as seen by the audience – be aware of this when describing performances you have seen!).

Tableau A frozen image carefully created in order to maximise the impact of a scene, originally used in Greek theatre to represent a violent act that occurred offstage. An *ekkyklema* (wheeled platform) would be brought out with the actors in a freeze upon it. In contemporary theatre, it is often used as a convention to imply the end of a scene as the lights fade but it is also a good rehearsal technique for focusing on character positions during key moments of action.

The Exploration of Drama and Theatre

Introduction

In this unit you are required to interpret **two** plays, designated by your teacher, through practical exploration, wider reading and research. The lessons that you have with your teacher should involve practical work, discussion and research for each of your two plays. We will discuss four plays here, but don't worry if your chosen play isn't discussed. All the approaches that are suggested for the example plays could be applied to any play text that you are studying, especially if they are written in a similar style or genre. Use the sections on each of the plays to create questions on and approaches to the texts you are studying.

When you are working on your two chosen texts, remember that the purpose of this unit is to get you to think about drama and theatre in a way that will really help you later on in the course when you begin realising and reviewing plays. This unit aims to bring you, through practical work, into contact with different approaches to writing, rehearsing and performing as well as directing, designing and acting.

You will be assessed in two areas: practical work and exploration work. Let's look at each of these in turn.

Practical work

Since you will be assessed throughout your practical work, the contributions that you make to your class lessons – through responses, group work, rehearsal work and performing work – are very important. Try to be positive throughout this unit, and bring enthusiasm to the practical sessions by making an effort to contribute as much as you can. You will be marked on the following areas of your practical work:

Subject matter and its treatment. You will be expected to show that you understand the potential that the play has in performance, and how you can make choices about its treatment through practical work.

Characterisation. Your practical work will explore how the characters of the play could be interpreted and you will need to be able to justify why you would do it in your chosen way.

Interpretation of meaning. You will demonstrate your practical interpretation of a few selected key moments from the play, and you will be expected to be able to show how meaning is being communicated to the audience through the performance.

Applying physical actions to the text. You will need to demonstrate clearly how to block a section of the play, and explain why it could be blocked in your chosen way. You will also be expected to demonstrate ways of approaching the text to create the

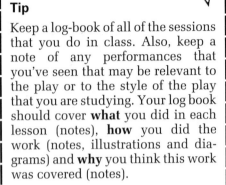

Tip

Keep a log-book of all of the sessions that you do in class. Also, keep a note of any performances that you've seen that may be relevant to the play or to the style of the play that you are studying. Your log book should cover **what** you did in each lesson (notes), **how** you did the work (notes, illustrations and diagrams) and **why** you think this work was covered (notes).

Further reading

As a starting point, try exploring the ideas and practice of important theatre practitioners such as Stanislavski, Brecht, Artaud, Brook and Grotowski, and see if their approaches could be applied to your chosen plays in rehearsal and performance. See the Understanding Theatre chapter for information on Stanislavski, Brecht and Artaud.

vocabulary of the physical actions needed for the play in performance.

Vocalising the text. You will need to demonstrate a variety of vocal techniques and styles, and show you can use these together with relevant text and action from the play. You'll explore the relationship between words or sounds, and how the way in which they are delivered can be used to create significance and meaning.

Exploration work

Your **exploration notes** are a very important series of notes that you will complete once your practical sessions are over. It's a good idea to keep a log of all of the sessions you take part in, and then use this log to help you put together your final notes. Remember that your response should always be in note form; this is not supposed to be an essay. Your notes could be in bullet points, bubble charts, flow diagrams or any other clear way of giving your response to the headings given in the margin. Here are some general guidelines:

> Your notes should always be clear. Make sure that even though they may be based around diagrams, they are still easy to read and to follow. They can be handwritten or word processed.

> Plan your notes well before you start putting them down on your final sheet of paper.

> Use the log that you have created during the course of all your practical work.

> Divide the sheet up into sections so that you know where you are going to write the responses for each element.

> Ask yourself questions about the play, and about how you tackled certain problems in rehearsal and performance. This will help you to shape your answers.

Your notes should consist of up to two sides of A4 paper or one side of A3 paper on each of the following headings:

✦ Contextualising the play
✦ Plot and sub-plot
✦ Use of language
✦ Form and structure
✦ Visual, aural and spatial elements.

Plot and sub-plot

You will have to outline clearly the plot of each play that you've studied. The plot does not just mean the story of the play – it is how the playwright has decided to construct the story, or the chronological series of events. There is always the possibility, of course, that the plot will not be chronological, or even in a sequence of any logical kind. The play may begin with the end of the story, as in Willy Russell's *Blood Brothers*. It may even decide to work backwards, as in Harold Pinter's *Betrayal*. You may find it easier to understand what is meant by plot by thinking of films such as *Sliding Doors* or *Pulp Fiction*, in which the story is told through a complicated plot, instead of a series of chronological scenes.

Sub-plot generally refers to a second, underlying story running through the play, though not all plays have one. It may feature the same characters as the main plot, different characters, or a mix of the two. It is often a story that makes some comment on the main plot by reflecting its action or themes. The relationship between plot and sub-plot is often clearly exemplified in Shakespeare's plays. For instance, in *A Midsummer Night's Dream*, the plot is carried by two different groups of characters: the Lovers in the main plot and the Mechanicals in the sub-plot. The Fairy characters move between the two plots. Both the main plot and the sub-plot are concerned with love: the Lovers and their relationships, and the Mechanicals and the play that they are trying to rehearse.

Use of language

You will have to identify the different types of language used in the play – by whom? when? – and why the playwright has chosen to use them. The language of the play concerns how the play's meaning is communicated to the audience through the characters. This can be through dialogue between characters or through a monologue delivered to the audience, or one character may speak their thoughts aloud as a soliloquy. The style of the language may be naturalistic, stylised, representative or poetic.

Form and structure

The form of the play refers to how the story is told through chosen sequences of events, and the style in which it could be performed. You will have to explain the reasoning behind the chosen conventions and devices of the play and refer to the way in which the playwright wants the story to be told. For example, the action of the play could be told through naturalistic scenes reflecting on everyday life, or through scenes that are clearly representative of events, or with stylised physical-theatre action using movement and music. The structure of a play refers to how the action of the play is put together, and how the scenes are linked. The scenes could flow continuously and chronologically, or they could be broken up and told in episodes. This difference is part of the distinction between dramatic and epic theatre.

Refer to the section on Brecht (page 17) for more on epic theatre.

Visual, aural and spatial elements

By visual, aural and spatial elements, we mean how the play looks, sounds and moves in performance. This concerns the function of the set, lighting and sound design and the symbolic effect they can have, as well as the decisions that can be made by a director when staging the play. In general, visual refers to the set, lighting and costumes; aural refers to the sound and the music; spatial refers to the staging. You will need to discuss all of these aspects of the play and talk in depth about two or three specific key moments or examples. Think about how the play looks and sounds, and how the space is used. You will need to consider set design, lighting and sound, as well as how the play can be directed to allow blocking of the actors and movement. It is often easy to confuse set and staging. The set is the design of the fixed space, and staging is how the director moves the actors around within this space.

Remind yourself who is responsible for each of these elements: the set is the responsibility of the designer; lighting is the responsibility of the lighting designer; costumes are the responsibility of the costume designer; sound is the responsibility of the sound designer, composer and/or musicians; and the staging is the responsibility of the director.

Contextualising the play

Contextualising refers to your understanding of the background of the play, and requires you to do some research. You will need to find out about the playwright, when the play was written, and why it was written. It would also be helpful to find out about other plays being performed at the time it was written, and also what was going on in the country at the time, so that you can establish whether the play has any political significance.

Sample exploration notes

On the following two pages you will find samples of exploration notes for two different plays, to suggest some ideas of how to approach your own notes. Around the edge there are comments on the strengths and weaknesses of these notes. Since you may not be familiar with these plays, short plot summaries have been added to aid your understanding of the student notes.

Form and Structure: *Equus* by Peter Shaffer

Equus is the story of a boy who blinded a stable of horses. Although it is his story the play is concerned with, it is revealed through a series of interviews with a psychiatrist called Dysart. It is through the eyes of Dysart that we learn of the case and meet with the boy. The case itself has a serious impact on the life of Dysart and this is why he tells us the story.

Annotation boxes (right side)

It is important that you identify the effect each form might have on the audience.

A good clear response that includes some practical experience. A new form – narration – is introduced but is not explored, which seems to imply the writer doesn't really know why narration is used.

The writer has done well to identify this form, since it is important to the style of the play, but this must be supported with textual or practical examples.

A strong concluding statement that links the different ideas to the themes and issues of the play.

Annotation boxes (left side)

This is an excellent start to the response. Key theatrical terms are used and the writer demonstrates a real understanding of the structure of the play.

This is a good personal reaction to the play. Trust your own thoughts rather than trying to search for the right answer.

Organising your thoughts into subheadings is an easy way of showing you understand the key areas. It's also a good way of checking you haven't missed anything.

It is good to mention that you have explored the text practically. However, this example is too brief. Specific details are needed saying why it was difficult.

Student response

Structure

The structure of the play is fairly CHRONOLOGICAL and EPISODIC but some flashbacks are used to reveal the detail of the story. The episodes of the treatment of the boy are told in the chronology that they happen, but the episodes themselves flash back to an earlier time in the boy's life. This creates a very complicated structure of a story within a story within a story and a complicated time frame of being in and out of time. This reminded me of a detective story as Dysart is trying to find out why Alan blinded the horses. The focus is not only on the crime but also on the mind of the detective.

directly with the boy. The conflict between the two protagonists can be tense or humorous but the intimate nature of the scenes highlights their developing relationship.

3. Dialogue and scene depiction through flashback: Shaffer often uses flashback in the middle of a duologue as a way of revealing the past. Dysart leads the scene through questions while one of the other characters takes the role of narrator and performer. In lessons, we rehearsed scenes 29 and 30, which looked at the moment in the cinema. While watching other groups performing, I realised how fun it is as an audience to see the focus switch from Dysart in the present to the father in the past. The narration was also effective.

4. Stylised representation of events: This is done through ritualistic movement, music and stylised physical theatre. The horses are represented through this form, as are the events where the boy encounters the horses.

The varied form of the play allows the text to deal with not only the relationships between people and our inner struggle, but also the more ritualistic and religious context of the play.

Form

The episodes of the play are extremely varied but can be split into four main areas.

1. Direct address monologues: Dysart, the psychiatrist, speaks directly to the audience, revealing his emotional state. I found this really difficult to act.

2. Dialogue with the boy: This is where we flash back to scenes in which the psychiatrist is talking and dealing

Visual, Aural and Spatial Elements: *Popcorn* by Ben Elton

Oscar-winning film director Bruce Delamitri is taken hostage, along with his Playboy-model girlfriend, at his luxurious home in Beverley Hills by two of America's most-wanted murderers. The criminal duo have been on a killing spree and, in the knowledge that they will soon be caught, try to force the responsibility for their actions on Delamitri and the violence in his films.

Set: The piece will be staged end-on, with the audience sat in straight rows facing the action. This formal seating encourages them to judge the actions of the characters and will also remind them of how they sit in the cinema during the filmed sequences, creating a link between the two forms.

The set should be realistic with lots of detail to show how rich Bruce is.

The large sofa deliberately dominates the set. It is an image of luxury, although it should also look impractical. It definitely is not comfortable and when Scout and Wayne hold them hostage the sofa should emphasise their feeling of being trapped.

Other Design Elements: The projection screen will be used during Act 2 when the image from the film crew is projected from behind. The cast will stare out to the audience implying that the actual television screen is downstage.

Theatrical blood will be in bags taped underneath the actors' clothing. When shots are fired, the actors will grab the bags in apparent pain, causing the bags to explode.

Costume: Since the play is set in the present all characters will wear modern dress suitable for their characters.

Lighting: The set will be brightly lit for most of the time although key scenes will need different effects.

During Bruce's Oscar acceptance speech he should be positioned stage right, away from the house, and lit from above with a profile isolating him in a pool of light, just as his style of film-making has isolated him from other members of the industry.

When the video sequences are used the lights need to be dimmed so that the projected images can be seen.

Sound: Speakers will be located on either side of the stage and behind the audience. The latter would only be used during Act 2 when the helicopters are circling overhead.

During Scene 2 and at the start of Scene 4, Scout and Wayne will wear microphones.

I would begin Act 1 with the stage in darkness. Violent sounds - bullets, screams and explosions - would be heard as the lights slowly fade up to reveal Karl, Bruce and Velvet. This would allow the images of 'Ordinary Criminals' to be created in the audience's mind.

Projector
Projection screen
Staircase leading to upstairs bedrooms
Wall mounted intercom
Flats painted to represent the walls of Bruce's lounge
Table with telephone
Sofa
Glass coffee table
Audience

Annotations:

This could be a lot more detailed, explaining exactly how his wealth is shown through design. Expensive looking materials such as chrome and leather could be used, while pictures of Bruce himself, perhaps in a copy of an Andy Warhol design, would show his narcissism. What colour are the walls? What effect is on the floor?

Try to specify the colour of the light. A pale yellow or straw coloured gel would make the house feel warm. A pale blue or steel coloured gel would create a cold atmosphere. There's even an argument for having more pretentious lighting effects with bright colours being projected onto the walls.

An excellent point linking design to intended audience impact.

It's good that a practical problem is identified, although more information could be given about exactly how and when this would happen.

A good point that links the action on stage to the impact on the audience.

This is a weak generalised statement which doesn't give any practical details about costume. If you are artistic, you could include designs. If you are by no means essential. Simple statements about style and colour would demonstrate an understanding as long as all decisions are justified.

This is an interesting point but the candidate doesn't explain why. Clearly they have an idea but it needs to be justified, for example: 'During this scene the audience need to believe it is an excerpt from a film and the amplified voices through the speakers will help to create this effect.'

☑ Exploration Notes checklist

There are six marks available for each question, and each response must be no longer than two sides of A4 or one side of A3. In order to receive five or six marks you will need to create work that demonstrates a very strong understanding of that aspect of both plays. It is important that you try to ensure your answers in each section are of an equally high standard. If your plot analysis is extremely detailed for one play but quite brief for the other, for example, you will not be able to attain the highest mark.

Use this checklist when organising your response to each area. Always remember that each play will have unique qualities that do not fit into a generic framework. Use this as a guide, but trust your own theatrical instinct and include any ideas that you think are relevant.

Plot and sub-plot

☐ Provide a clear outline of the plot. This could be written in prose or could be 'presented' in the form of a storyboard or a series of newspaper headlines.

☐ Identify the sub-plot, if there is one, and explain its purpose.

☐ Select two features of the plot and discuss their importance. These features could relate to the themes or the structure of the play.

Use of language

☐ Make sure you have identified at least three different styles of language used in the piece. In some plays, each character will have a different style. In others, you will need to look closely at the way in which the play is written and find a term to define the nature of the language.

☐ Support each use of language with at least one quotation from the text.

☐ Explain how that language might work in performance.

☐ Give practical examples from your own experience or suggest how you would direct the extract.

☐ State how voice and movement should be used.

Remember that subtext is an important aspect of the use of language in some plays.

☐ Discuss the intended impact of the language: why was it used and what effect might it have on an audience?

Form and structure

☐ Describe the structure of the piece: is the play separated into acts and scenes? Does the length vary? Is it written in chronological order? Does the structure of the play remind you of anything?

☐ Summarise the different forms used in the play and explain why the playwright chose this range.

☐ Identify three different forms and explore each of them in some detail.

☐ Include examples of practical work.

☐ State the effect that each of these forms would have in performance.

Visual, aural and spatial elements

☐ Give a general overview of the style of the piece and the demands that it places on the designer.

☐ Draw a set diagram including audience position.

☐ State why you have chosen to stage the piece in this manner.

☐ Identify key elements of the costume and explain what they might reveal about the characters and the demands of the piece.

☐ Explain what lighting will be used and the reasons for your choice.

☐ Outline your decisions on sound and relate them to their impact on the audience.

☐ Give at least one example of how the design elements relate to the performance of a scene or section.

Contextualising the play

☐ Research the playwright. Is this play typical of his or her work?

☐ How is the material influenced by social upbringing or specific experiences in life?

☐ Look at the genre of the piece. Is this a good example of the genre or does it break certain rules? Why was this genre successful? Would a modern audience be able to relate to it? How would a contemporary production differ from the original performance conditions? You may include references to other plays you have seen or read.

☐ Was the playwright influenced by any of the practitioners mentioned in the Understanding Theatre chapter? What similarities can you identify?

☐ Identify the themes and issues of the play. Explore how these ideas have evolved over time. Has society's reaction changed?

Make sure each idea is closely related to the text of the play. Irrelevant facts from a biography of the playwright will not demonstrate an understanding of the play.

Oedipus Rex

Oedipus Rex is the Latin translation of the Greek name for the play. You may also see it referred to as *Oedipus Tyrannus* and *Oedipus the King*.

Each spring, as part of the festival of Dionysus in Athens, three playwrights competed, each producing four plays: three tragedies and a satyr play.

Oedipus Rex by Sophocles is a Greek tragedy written approximately 427–426 BCE. Today, Sophocles is probably the most famous and successful of all Greek playwrights. He was born near Athens in 496 BCE into a wealthy family. At the age of 28, he competed for the first time in the City Dionysia and by his death in 406 BCE at the age of 90, he had won at this festival an incredible 24 times.

During his life, he wrote at least 123 plays but only seven have survived to the present day. He is credited with being the first Greek playwright to use three actors, which enabled him to explore his ideas in a more complex form. This meant that the role of the chorus was slightly less pronounced and allowed for more interaction, engagement and tension between characters.

When you read through the play for the first time make sure you read the introduction and the stage directions, as these will help you with your exploration notes. After the first reading of this or any text you should consider the following issues:

✦ What happens in the story? List the events in the order that they happen.

✦ How is the story told? Think about the structure and the form – the devices and conventions used.

✦ Are there any stage directions? Do they help when considering the form of the play?

✦ What immediate problems do you find when thinking about taking the words off the page and putting action on the stage?

Contextualising the play

Sophocles was a well-respected social figure in Athens with military experience. He was passionately religious and had a strong belief in moral values. He was a loyal citizen, although as he grew older he became cynical about the new democratic government that was being developed. One of his many strengths was his ability to explore complex human thoughts, emotions and desires through drama. Characters in his plays were thought to contain universal truth, demonstrating patterns of behaviour that audiences could recognise in themselves. His central characters are known for being strong-willed individuals who, against the backdrop of a glorious past, are confronted with great personal disaster.

The relatively simple structure of *Oedipus Rex* combined with its formal tone may initially suggest that it is a piece of historic theatre with little significance for the modern world. However, the style of leadership demonstrated by Oedipus in his opening speech is similar to the rhetoric used by many political figures today. The references to religion may have less relevance, although comparisons can be drawn to contemporary beliefs on fate and destiny.

The infamy of Oedipus' tale means that there is a wide range of sources over a range of periods to explore. Think of your work as a scrapbook of ideas about the play and the story. Cut and paste different source material and then add your own annotations. Look at images as well as text and be careful not to let one source dominate. Remember that personal analysis is essential.

Look at the role of religion in *Oedipus Rex*. Which gods are mentioned in the play? Would their significance be lost in a contemporary production? How might modern western views on religion alter the perception of certain characters and scenes? Focus on the concept of fate and destiny versus choice and free will. Theoretically, Oedipus was damned from birth, yet was there any chance he could have survived? Are there any similar concepts in today's society?

Oedipus' love for himself was greater than for his country. His hubris, or extreme self-belief, was ultimately his downfall. Modern-day politicians often tread a fine line between being strong leaders and appearing arrogant. Look at how George W. Bush and Tony Blair reacted to the 9/11 attack on New York, and the subsequent wars in Afghanistan and Iraq. Is too much self-belief a weakness? Consider what comments a performance of *Oedipus* could make to today's society about someone falling from a

---

Be careful when discussing stage directions for plays that are not modern. No ancient manuscripts of Sophocles' plays included stage directions and those you find in your text have been added by editors and translators. Try comparing different translations of *Oedipus Rex* to see how they vary.

Further study

Find out more about the festival of Dionysus. Look at the structure of the event and its religious and social significance to the people of Athens.

Further study

Sigmund Freud developed the theory of the Oedipus complex as a way of explaining the love a child might feel towards one parent while experiencing hate for the other. Look at this theory in more detail, tracking its relevance and influence. See, for example, www.freudfile.org.

Hubris means more than just 'pride': it means having so much belief in yourself that you overstep, often violently, the limits that as a human being you should remain within, thus offending the gods.

position of greatness. Does society get pleasure from watching people fall in this way?

Greek rhetorician Gorgias (483–378 BCE) stated that tragedy is about the emotional experience of the audience. Fear and pity are two important emotions in any tragedy. Aristotle believed that tragedy should contain actions that are capable of awakening 'pity for the undeserving sufferer and fear for the man like ourselves' in order to have the greatest impact on an audience.

Aristotle (384–322 BCE) is probably the most influential of all Greek philosophers. His writings covered all major areas of thought, including science, ethics, politics and art, and his views on drama were particularly influential on later scholars. In his opinion, Sophocles' *Oedipus Rex* was the finest example of a tragedy.

 Re-read the section of *Oedipus* from the Messenger's speech to the end. Make a list of moments which elicit our pity for Oedipus and moments where we might fear for ourselves. Which list is longer? Would it be possible to evoke this response from an audience in a contemporary production?

Web link

A useful website showing reviews and photographs of the 1988 production of *Greek* is www.agirlwholovesbrucepayne.com /greekjune2002.html. *Greek* was later turned into an opera by Mark Antony Turnage. What is it about the story that invites this treatment?

Steven Berkoff adapted *Oedipus*, renaming it *Greek*. He set it in London, using cockney caricatures, and translated the original plague into images of acid rain, deforestation, football hooliganism and AIDS. The central character, Eddy, is warned of his fate by a fortune teller but he seems to have a lot more control over his destiny than Oedipus. Berkoff criticises the inertia that he sees in society, and the language he uses is violent and designed to shock. Read the play and note the choices Berkoff has made in adapting *Oedipus*. Is such an adaptation necessary for a contemporary society?

Plot and sub-plot

Thebes is gripped by a devastating plague. Oedipus, the ruler of Thebes, has already rid the city of the sphinx, a monster with the head of a woman on the body of a lion who sat at the gate of Thebes and asked riddles of those trying to pass, killing all who failed to answer correctly. He now insists he will find the cause of the plague. He consults the oracle of the god Apollo and is told that he must find the killer of Laius, the former king of Thebes. Oedipus publicly curses the murderer and proclaims that he will stop at nothing until the truth about Laius' murder is known. As the action unfolds, segments of the past are slowly revealed, allowing Oedipus to finally realise that *he* is '...the unclean thing/The dirt that breeds disease'. He was the murderer of Laius, unaware that the man was his father. It becomes clear that his wife is also his mother, and she kills herself in shame. Horrified, Oedipus blinds himself, and Creon, his brother-in-law, banishes him from the city.

According to legend, the sphinx asked Oedipus, 'What walks on four legs in the morning, two legs at noon, and three legs in the evening?' He correctly answered that it is man, who as a baby crawls on all fours and in old age uses a stick as a third leg. In frustration that he had solved her riddle, the sphinx threw herself from the city walls.

The majority of the action in *Oedipus Rex* takes place before the play begins. The interest lies in how Oedipus discovers the truth about who he is and what he has done. Think of it as a detective story where the clues gradually reveal the murderer: the first task is to unravel the different strands of the story into a clear chronological order.

 Create a timeline of events, starting with Laius learning of the oracle's prophecy and finishing with Oedipus' banishment. Since this will immediately demonstrate that you have a command of the different strands of the plot, you should include this in your final exploration notes.

Working in groups of three or four, divide the script into a series of scenes. Using a maximum of 20 words for each scene, write down a sentence which describes the action. For example, the opening section could be summed up as: 'Oedipus addresses the people of Thebes and insists he will save them from the plague.'

Once you have done this, direct each other into a still image that epitomises the emotion and action in this scene. Think about whether including the chorus will make the image stronger or weaker. Now choose one of the more powerful lines from the section you are working on and have the actor who is playing that character deliver the words. Repeat this process for each of your scenes.

Rehearse your ideas so that you create an abridged performance of the play. Follow the structure of image–sentence–quotation and then move to the next image. Try to ensure that all movement between scenes is carefully planned so that the work runs smoothly from one piece of action to the next.

By going through this process you can show that you have a clear command of the plot as well as demonstrating that you have the ability to describe it concisely and in some detail. This is essential if you are going to achieve high marks in this section. Try converting your practical work into a storyboard for a film or even a cartoon strip. The quality of your drawing is not important – it's perfectly acceptable to use stick-people to present your ideas.

In *Oedipus Rex*, there is no sub-plot as such, since all of the play's action revolves around the protagonist. However, it is worth looking at how the role of king is portrayed.

> The protagonist is the play's central character.

With a partner, read though the three exchanges between Creon and Oedipus. Focus on the first image of optimism as Creon enters looking happy and contrast this with the argument, and then with the end scene. How do the characters react to pressure, and are they equally strong in their decision-making? How does Creon in the last scene of the play compare with Oedipus at the start? What information is implied about Laius' leadership style? How has each king's leadership style affected the action of the play?

Web link

Many websites offer plot summaries and theme analyses that can help to clarify any grey areas. Try www.gradesaver.com/ClassicNotes/Titles/oedipus as a starting point and then work from the links provided.

Use of language

The style of the language within the play will depend on the translation you use. However, there are immediate features that should transcend all editions. Much of the language will be heightened and poetic, written in verse. There should be a clear difference between the strength of Oedipus' royal declamations at the start of the play and the words of the shepherd. Try to focus on the differences between the characters as this will provide a starting point for your analysis.

> The translation used in this section is by Don Taylor (Methuen 1986).

> Heightened language is more formal speech which can, on occasions, appear unrealistic. The words are carefully chosen by the playwright to ensure maximum impact.

The language of *Oedipus Rex* works on two levels: the words spoken by the characters and the images created on stage. At the beginning of the play these work in unison. Oedipus enters through the palace doors. He speaks like a great orator and his movement should be confident in order to reflect his obvious power.

Individually, rehearse the opening 11 lines, finishing on 'Everyone knows my name'. Consider how vocal and physical work could ensure Oedipus' character has maximum impact at the start of the play. Now, in groups of four or five, perform this section to each other, identifying specific moments where the communication of his greatness is most successful. Write these down in your exploration notes.

As the play progresses, the power in Oedipus' voice should be betrayed by the lack of control in his movement. Consider how physical and vocal language could be used to ensure the blind prophet Teiresias has more status then the king. Teiresias speaks in riddles and uses his vision to prophesy. Look closely at how his language baffles and threatens the powerful king, for example: 'I know, but you do not/ That the woman you love is not the woman you love.' In pairs, try positioning Teiresias centre-stage and consider how his stillness could be contrasted with the over-confident and arrogant movement of the king.

Look at the use of language between the shepherd who knows the truth and the desperate Oedipus. How is the scene written to ensure maximum impact on the audience? How would you emphasise the difference in their vocal delivery in performance?

The language of the chorus is much more evocative and poetic than that of the main characters and is essential in creating the world outside the play: the dying city, the influence of the gods and a sense of personal suffering. Their reactions to the actions and words of the protagonists are often important in guiding the response of the audience. Think carefully about how the chorus can work in a modern production. There is a danger in supporting their spoken words with literal gestures since these could appear trite and superficial. Instead focus on more abstract movements in order to create mood and atmosphere.

In groups of between six and eight, look at the first chorus section. Begin with 'Our agonies are beyond telling', and finish on 'Will you not answer our cry?'. Nominate someone to be the chorus leader who will read all of the section. Everyone else should individually underline eight short phrases from this section that they feel have impact, for example 'tearing their nails'. Now, the chorus leader should read the entire section while everyone else will only speak their chosen lines. This should create a random allocation of text with most lines being spoken by more than one member of the group. This immediately emphasises the size and range of the suffering of the people of Thebes.

Experiment with simple movements that aid the communication of this section of the text. The group should begin with their backs to the audience and only turn slowly to face them when they say their first line. Try rocking, swaying, standing in a tight group, in small groups or even individually. Record what you have learnt in your notes.

 In order for the audience to imagine fully the horrors of the offstage action, the messenger's language is brutal and activates powerful images in the mind. If delivered well, the language of the messenger speech can have an even greater impact on the audience than such events would if depicted on stage, as it plays on the resources of the audience's imagination. Photocopy a section of the speech and stick it in your exploration notes. Imagine you are directing the section. Annotate the text to show how you would want it to be performed. Try to identify changes of pace (including pause), tone, volume and emotion. Consider how vocal delivery might reinforce the power of key phrases.

Form and structure

The stylised nature of ancient Greek performance makes this a relatively easy section to explore. Essentially, most plays followed certain principles, which Aristotle discussed in his *Poetics*. It was the structure of *Oedipus Rex* in particular that led Aristotle to view the play as such a fine example of a tragedy, and his rules are largely based on this play. Although the idea of reading Aristotle may sound daunting, it is actually a clear, insightful and short introduction to the rules of theatre and his ideas have been echoed in Shakespeare as well as in the work of many modern playwrights. Essentially he stressed the importance of the dramatic unity of action, so that the play is properly focused and avoids distractions. Later writers elaborated on Aristotle's own ideas and offered a rule that plays ought to possess three dramatic unities – time, place and action:

> **Time.** All events must take place in chronological order. The running time of the performance must mirror the time we spend in the world of the play. Essentially *Oedipus Rex* happens in real time.

> **Place.** The play should be set in one location, putting the focus on plot and character development. *Oedipus Rex* is set in the royal courtyard, outside the palace of Oedipus in Thebes.

> **Action.** The action in the play must be consequential and rational. Aristotle criticised 'episodic' plays, which consist of a series of episodes that do not follow on rationally from one to another, requiring the audience to believe in an unlikely turn of events or coincidence.

Since the play is chronological and the locale is constant, the key area to focus on is action. Oedipus is a tragic character because he falls from a position of greatness as a result of the tragic flaw in his character: hubris.

 Try charting Oedipus' downfall on a graph noting how his high status falls over time. Label key moments of the action.

Web link

You can find the text of Aristotle's *Poetics* at www.authorama.com/the-poetics-1.html.

The exception to this is the choral odes, during which much time could occur off-stage.

These 'three unities' are so frequently attributed to Aristotle himself that almost everyone in the theatre now believes them to be his idea. It is important that you demonstrate a knowledge of these unities in your exploration notes since they are a standard critical way of summing up how Sophocles built his play, and have been very influential on generations of playwrights.

Oedipus begins as a strong character. He is a king, a man we respect, and his initial speech increases his status. However, from the moment of Teiresias' entrance he loses power and his downfall begins, since his pride prevents him from accepting the words of the blind seer. Each new action serves to accelerate his descent. It is only when he emerges as a blind man, aware of his crimes, that he begins to regain our sympathy and some of his initial status.

Conversely, you could concentrate on Aristotle's division of the plot into reversal of situation, recognition and suffering.

> **Reversal of situation** is when a character bringing good news or information actually finds themselves bringing bad news and adding to the suffering of the central character, as with the messenger who reveals to Oedipus that the parents he has avoided for so long were not in fact his mother and father.

> **Recognition** happens when a character realises the full extent of their role in the tragedy, when all the detective work has been done. Both Jocasta and Oedipus have moments of recognition.

> The scene of **suffering** usually happens in the last episode where the protagonist is publicly humiliated and suffers for their actions. At this point, an audience should experience a form of catharsis.

The role of the chorus is vital in the play and its presence will clearly add to any production. It is possible to use it as a stylised image of man, where individual identities are ignored. However, there is more dramatic potential if you consider it as a group of 12–15 individuals who represent a cross section of the citizens of Thebes. They can speak or sing the text individually, in unison or in canon and their movement could be realistic or choreographed. Their role is to question, reject, reinforce and explore the behaviour of the protagonist, acting as a guide to lead us through the play.

? Look at their speech beginning 'Like a shadow thrown in the dust' immediately after the scene with Oedipus, the shepherd and the Corinthian. How do they make the audience re-evaluate the words and actions of characters? Consider how the questioning in this scene might contrast with the previous interrogation of characters. Use specific moments to illustrate your ideas and to explore their impact on an audience.

Stichomythia is a series of one-line exchanges that would often be spoken quickly in order to increase tension. The technique is used when Oedipus challenges both Teiresias and Creon. In pairs, choose one of these scenes and sit opposite each other. How could the mood and atmosphere be created solely through vocal work?

Visual, aural and spatial elements

It is important to remember that productions of plays in ancient Greece were part of a religious festival that all citizens would attend. In Athens, the Theatre of Dionysus would probably have held up to 14,000 people. The style of performance reflected the demands of such a space, with bold characterisation, masks and

---

Catharsis is the release or cleansing of emotional tensions. Such scenes were thought to help the audience become better citizens through the play, since they could experience extreme emotions in a controlled way. The idea was Aristotle's answer to Plato's hostility to tragedy, which he considered to encourage the wrong emotions and behaviour in its audience.

Sophocles is said to have increased the chorus from 12 to 15 members.

Web link

Read the parody of stichomythia in 'Fragment of a Greek tragedy' by the English poet and classical scholar A. E. Housman, available at http://ccat.sas.upenn.edu/jod/texts/housman.html

grand costumes aiding communication of ideas across the large semi-circular auditorium. Reducing the play to a traditional proscenium arch theatre or even a small studio space for a modern production can create problems, and it is therefore important that you remain clearly focused on the impact you are trying to achieve. Select the traditions of Greek theatre that you think best suit your interpretation, rather than slavishly regurgitating all of the traditional elements for the sake of demonstrating your knowledge of the past. Your notes should be a *personal* exploration.

In order to do justice to your design, you should use an A3 sheet that will allow you the flexibility to sketch, write and even stick on images that have influenced you. Remember that it is the ideas rather than the artistic quality that will gain you marks, although it is important that the presentation is clear. Be decisive. Say exactly how your production would be staged rather than giving alternatives as this can become confusing.

Consider the different possibilities of performing in proscenium arch, thrust, traverse, round and promenade theatres. Select one and base your design around this. For example, one end of a traverse stage could be the impressive palace while the other end implies the decaying city of Thebes.

It is generally believed that there was a raised stage at the back that separated the protagonists from the chorus, who remained on the large circular dancing area called the orchestra. The protagonists could move between the orchestra and the stage, which emphasised the social divide, but also the downfall from greatness. Would you wish to use such a platform in your design? How would Oedipus descend to the chorus at the end of the play?

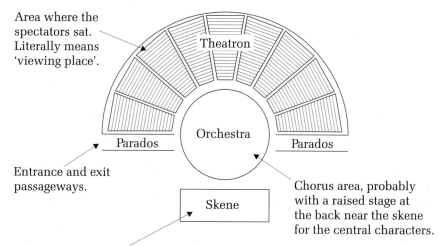

Area where the spectators sat. Literally means 'viewing place'.

Entrance and exit passageways.

The skene was a construction at the back of the orchestra representing the building outside which the play was set.

Chorus area, probably with a raised stage at the back near the skene for the central characters.

Spatially, the dynamic between the audience, the chorus and the protagonists is well worth exploring in this section. Should the chorus remain on stage, venture into the audience or even be above the seating area providing a link between mortals and the gods?

Web link

A useful website for getting more of an impression of ancient theatre is http://didaskalia.open.ac.uk/StudyArea/study.html

Staging

Sophocles is said to have been the first dramatist to introduce scene-painting to represent the setting.

Think about...

The injury to Oedipus' ankles, which were pinned when he was exposed as a baby, is referred to several times during the play and is said to be the reason for his name, which literally means 'swollen foot'. The shepherd notes that even all these years later, it is still obvious. Will you portray the king as limping or at all affected by the injury?

Lighting

Obviously, traditional performances were in the open air and used natural lighting. Would you look to recreate this realistic lighting or is a more stylised interpretation appropriate? Consider how shadows might be used to emphasise the theme of hidden truth.

Costume

Traditionally all main characters were performed by three actors who relied on the details in the mask and costume to distinguish between roles. Are your performers going to be masked or unmasked? Remember that you will have to present the blinded Oedipus in the final scene. Modern productions often use a mask for the bloodied eyes. If you do this, you will have to decide whether all your actors will wear masks throughout the play or whether you will just use a mask for this scene. Keep in mind that using masks ensures that emotion has to be portrayed entirely through means other than facial expression. Explain the reasons for making your choice. Does your costume suggest any particular period, ancient or modern, or allude to the spiritual elements of the play?

The portrayal of Teiresias can be problematic. The image of the blind prophet needs to be powerful and his dialogue with Oedipus needs to commence the king's downfall. How is this stage presence achieved?

The use of sound does not initially appear central to the piece, yet it could significantly aid the creation of mood and atmosphere. How could the sense of Thebes' plague be created? How might the grandness of Oedipus' entrance through the palace doors be exaggerated by sound? What instruments could be used incidentally to emphasise the action of particular scenes? Bear in mind that traditionally the chorus sang in Greek theatre, accompanied by instruments.

Further study

In Peter Hall's traditional production at the National Theatre in 1996, Teiresias was a ghostly white figure pulled on by a rope attached to his waist. Try to find pictures of this production on the Internet to generate ideas.

Norwegian romanticism was similar to melodrama in style (see page 38). A simplistic moral overtone dominated the play; good actions were rewarded and bad behaviour punished. For the 'well-made play', see page 59.

" Any tendency for the actors to congregate downstage should be avoided, and their relative positions on stage should change whenever it appears natural; generally, every scene and every visual image should be, as far as possible, a reflection of reality. "

Ibsen

A Doll's House

A Doll's House by Norwegian playwright Henrik Ibsen is a realist play that was written in 1879 in both Rome and Amalfi in Italy.

Throughout his life, Ibsen (1828–1906) struggled to be accepted by the Norwegian theatrical establishment. His reaction against the notions of romanticism and the contrived 'well-made' play meant that his works were initially dismissed. Consequently, he spent 27 years living abroad in Italy and Germany. When he wrote *A Doll's House*, he gained European recognition for the first time and it was this that paved his way for a return home.

Contextualising the play

The emotional journey Ibsen experienced in life is reflected in the complexity of his characters. His mother's over-reliance on religion and his father's depression are elements that recur throughout his writing. His acting style demanded a truthful performance that encouraged the audience to identify emotionally with the characters' internal states, rather than simply relying on physical gesture to convey feelings.

The psychologically realistic nature of *A Doll's House* and its exploration of individualistic ethics versus socially determined ethics makes it an excellent play to discuss in both a historical and a modern context. Ibsen's focus on human nature and its response to complex situations make this a text that is as relevant today as it has always been. Add to this the context of the feminist movement and the rights of women and you have a rich range of resources to draw on.

As always, it is important that you do not rely entirely on research. You need to consider the implications that all information has on the rehearsal and performance of the text. The nature of your response should play to your strengths. You may feel comfortable doing an essay-style response linking your ideas with both past and present productions. However, it is equally valid to produce an A3 collage of different thoughts and comments on a range of areas that you found most interesting. You need to discuss your points in detail.

Many of Ibsen's protagonists share common features. Essentially, they are members of a bourgeois family who appear to have lost direction in life. They have a choice to make: either they can continue in their current state of dutiful emptiness or they can elect a different way of living which may lead to self-discovery, but may also lead to loneliness or isolation. It is this conflict between the two states that forms the heart of his work.

Look at Ibsen's play *Ghosts* and the character Mrs Alving. What similarities are there with the role of Nora Helmer? How does Ibsen use these women to challenge the beliefs of society?

Ibsen was forced to write an alternative ending to *A Doll's House*. Nora's decision to leave her husband shocked the 19th-century audiences and the actress who took the role of Nora when the play toured Germany insisted that the ending be changed. In the amended script, just as Nora is about to leave, Torvald insists she take one last look at the children asleep and explains how they will wake the following morning motherless. The thought of leaving them is enough for her to abandon her plans and return to the role of doll wife. Consider how this might change the meaning of the play and why this outcome might have been demanded.

When discussing Torvald's behaviour, the critic Hemmer suggests: 'It is not the human being in him which speaks to Nora at their final confrontation, it is society and its institutions and authorities which speak through him.' What elements of Torvald's language in Act 3 could suggest he is indeed representing the common view of Norwegian society? Is this a fair perception of his character? Is he a tool for conveying this aspect of the playwright's message or is the role more complex than this? Consider how you might direct the actors during this section and what issues you would explore.

Web link

A good starting point for the discussion of themes and issues within the play is www.gradesaver.com/ClassicNotes/Titles/dollshouse
Remember, however, that using extracts of work from the Internet without identifying their practical significance will not earn you many marks and may count against you.

> These women of the modern age, mistreated as daughter, as sisters, as wives, not educated according to their talents, debarred from following their missions, deprived of their inheritance, embittered in mind – these are the ones who supply the mothers for the new generation. What will be the result?
>
> Ibsen

'Ibsen and the realistic problem drama' by Bjorn Hemmer, in *The Cambridge Companion to Ibsen* (Cambridge University Press 1994).

A more detailed discussion of Stanislavski's ideas can be found on page 8.

The translation used here is by Michael Meyer (Methuen 1985).

Further study

Look at Stanislavski's ideas and any links with Ibsen's views on theatre and explain how you might use them during a 21st-century production.

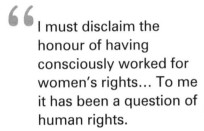

I must disclaim the honour of having consciously worked for women's rights… To me it has been a question of human rights.

> Ibsen, at a meeting of the Norwegian Association for Women's Rights.

The term for this is 'prior action'.

Many 20th-centry performances of the play are influenced by the work of Stanislavski, who aimed to ensure all performances conveyed a sense of emotional truth. He believed that the external actions of the characters needed to be balanced with internal feelings through a complex system of rehearsal.

In pairs, apply Stanislavski's techniques to the end of the play, beginning on Torvald's line 'May I write to you, Nora?'. Rehearse this extract looking specifically at objectives and emotion memory. Is it possible to convey his sense of loss? How hard is it to sympathise with his character? Perform the scene to the rest of the group and get feedback on the effectiveness of each portrayal. Draw some conclusions on the relevance of Torvald's character to males in contemporary society. Are today's men governed by a different set of social rules?

Plot and sub-plot

When her husband, Torvald, was gravely ill, Nora Helmer secretly borrowed money to fund a holiday in Italy to allow him time to recuperate. She repays the debt through regular instalments, using money she has saved from her allowance. However, when Torvald recovers and is made manager of the bank, his first task is to sack Krogstad, who coincidentally is the person who loaned Nora the money. This loan was falsely obtained, since Nora forged her father's signature, and Krogstad threatens to publicly embarrass both her and her husband unless she manages to get him his job back at the bank. Torvald refuses to be influenced by his wife and consequently the truth is revealed. His anger at his wife's actions is only calmed when the threat of blackmail is revoked but by this time Nora has realised that she never loved her husband and she leaves.

The main plot can be clearly identified as the relationship between Nora, Torvald and Krogstad. These three characters drive the action of the play. Begin your notes by focusing on them in isolation from the others, by making a list of all key plot developments, including action that happened before the play began.

Much of the tension that is created in performance relies on the audience reflecting on the language and actions of characters in previous scenes. In groups of three, using the list you have just made, find two scenes where Nora discusses the same issue first with Krogstad and then with Torvald. For example, in Act 1, look at how Nora confesses to Krogstad that she forged her father's signature and Torvald's explanation of Krogstad's previous misdemeanour: 'He forged someone else's name. Have you any idea what that means?' Choose short extracts from the different scenes and rehearse them in a way that might highlight the contrasting emotions of Nora. Perform the scenes to the rest of your group and ask them to comment on specific moments where the tension was at its greatest. In your exploration notes, discuss how these three characters' actions help to highlight the themes of the play. In this extract, for example, lies and deceit are emphasised particularly.

The main sub-plot is the relationship between Krogstad and Linde. The action of the play is cleverly structured to ensure they do not meet face to face until Act 3, but each character refers to the other in their opening scenes.

MRS LINDE Nora, who was that man? … It was him then … How he's changed.

And also:

KROGSTAD I saw your husband cross the street … with a lady … was not that lady a Mrs Linde?

 In pairs, focus on one of these scenes. Consider how you could subtly convey to an audience a sense of the emotion experienced by Linde or Krogstad. Remember, Linde might be embarrassed by her past actions and Krogstad would not want to show himself to be weak in front of Nora. Rehearse the extract, keeping movement to a minimum. Now try working on the opening of Act 3. Look at Ibsen's stage directions and try to create Linde's anxiousness. When Krogstad enters, he is clearly confused. Consider how this confusion might be performed. Experiment with him being aggressive, cold and cautious. In your notes, explore the role the sub-plot has in commenting on the main action within the play.

The critic Tornqvist suggested Nora and Linde were 'parallel figures moving in opposite directions'. Focus on the characters' relationships and the difference in how they start and end the play. Ibsen deliberately draws comparisons between characters and their situations. Both Krogstad and Nora forged signatures and both contemplated suicide. Torvald and Rank (for different reasons) both try to maintain an external image of calm despite their inner turmoil.

Further reading

Egil Tornqvist's book *Ibsen: A Doll's House* (Cambridge University Press 1995) is a detailed analysis of the play text and its impact through performance. The language is easy to read and he makes interesting points that you could refer to in your notes.

Select one or two such relationships and in your notes explore the comparisons and contrasts within them through specific reference to the text.

The children and the nurse seem inconsequential to the main plot yet their presence further highlights the ramifications of the other characters' actions. Think about how these characters might make the audience reflect on the action within the play.

Use of language

Although there are many different translations of the text, essentially they all remain true to Ibsen's original use of language. In order to write a good response, it is important that you identify the different styles used in the text and the impact they may have on the audience. However, you must remember that your notes are a record of how you have explored the text so try to support your ideas with practical examples from your work on the play or suggestions on how the language might be performed. You should be able to recognise the use of:

➤ Complex or simplistic language

➤ Heightened or poetic language

➢ Metaphor, imagery and symbolism

➢ Questions

➢ Pauses, different sentence lengths and changes in vocabulary

➢ Subtext (the meaning beneath the text)

➢ Characteristic words or phrases

➢ References to the natural world

➢ Specific patterns of speech for each character.

Remember this should be a personal exploration, so focus on the areas you find most interesting.

Try organising your ideas in table format. This will help you to identify the use of language and its effect. For example:

Use of language	Quotation	Practical application	Impact on audience
Frequent use of questions to highlight Torvald's confusion in Act 3.	'Nora, what kind of way is this to talk?' 'What kind of way is this to describe our marriage?' 'Nora, how can you be so unreasonable and ungrateful?'	Both characters sit formally at table centre stage. Nora to hold eye contact but to use gestures sparingly, implying her control. Torvald is clearly uncomfortable sitting down and talking seriously. With each question, his vocal tone should become increasingly desperate, with less fluency in his delivery.	The contrast between the characters should be immediately evident. Torvald's questioning is an attempt to regain his status but his desperation only serves to reinforce how he is lost and confused.

Nora uses language to manipulate the male characters in the play with varying degrees of success. Working in groups of four, choose three moments where Nora is alone on stage with Krogstad, Torvald and Rank. Find a quotation that highlights how she tries to manipulate the characters in each scene. Sit each of the male characters on a chair and consider how the manner in which they sit communicates how they respond to the manipulation. Try acting each of the lines, thinking carefully about the tone of voice used and the stress put on certain words. How does Nora's proximity to the characters affect the power of her manipulation? Comment on what you have learnt about her language in your notes.

Focus on the difference between Torvald and Rank. Make a list of the phrases Torvald uses to refer to his wife. What do you think references to animals in the natural world might suggest to an audience about their relationship? Now look at the scenes with Rank and how Nora appears to be in control. Draw comparisons between sentence length, vocabulary, use of pause and questions. Does either character change their use of language when their status changes?

A Doll's House is often considered to be a transitional play, between the sensationalism of melodrama and realism. Krogstad, in particular, is a character who could fit comfortably in both genres. On one hand, he is the stereotypical villain, making threats and discussing the horrors of suicide. However, he could also be considered to be a victim of circumstance who has been hurt by Linde and needs his job to survive in the cruel world.

 Make a list of the key phrases that Krogstad uses and suggest how they could be performed in both a melodramatic and a realistic style.

Form and structure

The structure of the play obeys many of the guidelines associated with the philosopher Aristotle's discussion of Greek tragedy. The unities of place and action are followed and the only interruptions to time are the natural divisions at the end of each act. Ibsen uses the break to move the audience forward to the next moment of tension and the focus on the 60 hours or so during the Christmas period adds particular impact when the play revolves so much around money, hidden secrets and family.

Ibsen's structure is further influenced by the concept of the 'well-made play'. This was a common structure in the 19th century and was made famous by Eugene Scribe (1791–1861) who used the format to develop nearly 500 plays. There are many rules that govern the nature of such a play, but essentially the action can be broken into three simple sections: exposition, development and denouement.

> The **exposition** reveals the facts of the situation. Act 1 in *A Doll's House* introduces all the main characters, outlines past events and provides a context for future action.

> The **development** is sometimes referred to as the 'complication', since new information is introduced that makes the protagonist's situation more difficult. Rank's confession of his true feelings and Krogstad's dismissal followed by his posting of the letter all take place in Act 2, heightening Nora's emotional turmoil.

> The **denouement** is the unravelling of the plot, dealing with each of the strands of the play and leading the audience to a natural conclusion. Ibsen does bring together the different strands – Krogstad and Linde talk, Rank announces his death, metaphorically thanking Nora 'for the light' she has brought to his life, and Torvald and Nora talk about the issues raised within the play. However, it is not a natural conclusion; it is a discussion that leads to an unpredictable future for Nora and her family. The playwright encourages the audience to hypothesise about what might happen in the future.

 In your notes, write down the headings 'exposition' (Act 1), 'development' (Act 2) and 'denouement' (Act 3). Examine the three areas of the play and use quotations from the text to highlight how Ibsen uses the well-made play structure. Look at how Act 3 in particular appears to lull the audience into thinking that everything will be resolved.

The dominant form of the play is **duologue**, a conversation between two individuals. Ibsen repeatedly uses two characters to highlight the

Look at the form and structure of *Oedipus Rex* described on page 51. Draw comparisons between the structures of the two tragedies.

Web link

A useful discussion of Scribe and the elements he used is given at www.wayneturney.20m.com/scribe.htm

Denouement is originally a French word meaning 'undoing a knot'. Compare it with the Aristotelian idea of recognition: see page 52.

moral conflict of each scene. Even when the characters superficially appear to be in agreement, the conflict should be conveyed through the subtext. For example, when Nora dominates the first conversation with Mrs Linde, the latter should show frustration at her frivolous nature. Because duologue dominates, when Ibsen chooses to use different forms their impact on the audience is increased.

 Get into groups of three or four. Each member of the group should choose one of Nora's soliloquies. Rehearse them as an ensemble performance that highlights the confusion in Nora's mind. Try overlapping or repeating words. Consider how the size and speed of physical actions might convey character. Is there a logical development in her words that shows an emotional progression throughout the play or are the thoughts independent of time?

The name of the tarantella dance stems from the Italian town Taranto where they believed the only cure for the bite of a tarantula was a frenzied dance that would leave the participant exhausted but cured.

Web link

A sample of tarantella music can be found at www.sicilianculture.com/folklore/tarantella.htm.

More information about how to perform the dance is available at www.streetswing.com/histmain/z3tartla.htm.

The use of dance and music through the tarantella scene at the end of Act 2 is an interesting device in a realistic play. On the most basic level, Nora uses it to prevent Torvald from going to the letter box and discovering Krogstad's letter. Symbolically, however, it is extremely significant.

Consider why Ibsen chose to use the tarantella as a device. What does the history of the dance say about the marriage? How does it reflect Nora's mental state? Remember that Italy was where Torvald was taken to recover from his illness and is the source of Nora's financial difficulties; the dance and her costume are constant reminders of this.

Visual, aural and spatial elements

In order to bring *A Doll's House* to life, you need to consider how it might work in a three-dimensional space. Visual elements will include the environment of the Helmers' house as well as the costume and make-up worn. The spatial elements will include staging, traditionally the proscenium arch, and the size of the performance space. In addition, subtle use of music and sound effects may add to the changes in mood of the piece. Remember, unless there are two intervals, you will need to indicate the passing of time between two acts. Consider how the sound of the final door slamming could be amplified to ensure maximum effect.

This is the most creative of the written sections and is a real chance for you to explore fully the practical implications of the play. Don't panic if you can't draw. Straight lines and two-dimensional drawings are perfectly acceptable. At the beginning of Act 1, Ibsen gives very specific information about the staging of the play. It is possible to begin your design by following his instructions. However, you do not need to mirror his ideas. You could choose to stage your play in the round. Consequently, the positioning of the different seating areas will need to be carefully considered to ensure balance. Use an A3 sheet to present your ideas and illustrate your stage design in the middle. This will act as a focal point, with all of your other comments about visual, aural and spatial elements placed round the outside.

Props

Ibsen gave considerable thought to the use of visual symbols to add resonance to the action and to explore facets of the characters. Look at the role of stage props in the play – behind every object on stage there lies a meaning. The stove is a symbol of warmth that certain characters could gather around when trying to forget the harsh realities of the cold world outside the house. The macaroons highlight Nora's deceitful nature at the start of the play, since she eats one in front of the audience and yet tells her husband she didn't stop at the cake shop. The Christmas tree is in many ways a metaphor for Nora herself. She enters with it at the start, but hides it from her husband. It is centre stage at the end of Act 1, where it is prettified to highlight the happiness of their home, but is stripped and dishevelled in Act 2. How might these elements influence the use of stage space in particular moments of action?

[?] How might the image of a doll's house be created? What style of furniture, windows, fabric might help to emphasise this theme? Many doors are suggested by the text so think about entrances and exits. Both the entrance from the hall and the door to Torvald's study are essential focal points during the performance. How might they be used to increase tension?

Costume

Consider the costume of the characters. What colour, style and fabric would best suit your performance? Are the costumes detailed and realistic or are small pieces of costumes used to symbolise character? Consider how the costumes change as each of the characters changes. How does Torvald's appearance in Act 1 contrast with Act 3? When Nora states 'I've changed', how might her costume reflect the psychological change that has taken place?

Sound

How might sound contribute to the play? Consider the tarantella music, the door slam and the sense of the party continuing upstairs. In a non-naturalistic presentation, consider how music might underscore the monologues. If you are highlighting Nora's doll-like behaviour, this could be achieved through the sound of a music box or a violin playing pizzicato.

Lighting

Lighting could be essentially realistic, with warm (straw) general covers of lighting used in the majority of scenes. However, the use of the light in Act 2 with Rank and Nora implies a reduction in intensity. You may also wish to isolate Torvald at the end of the play and consider how lights shining through lattice windows might imply a cage or cell.

Metamorphosis

Stephen Berkoff (b. 1937) is a great advocate of stirring and using the audience's imagination to get them fully engaged and involved in the play, rather than sitting back in a passive manner with all of their thinking done for them.

Contextualising the play

Kafka

Metamorphosis is an unusual play text because it is the dramatisation of a short novel by a different author. The story was written in German by Franz Kafka (1883–1924) in 1912 and it was published years later. There are various areas of his life that have a direct relevance to the play. He was born into a German-speaking Jewish family in Prague, which was then part of an Austrian-Hungarian empire. He was dominated by his father, who never really accepted Kafka's talents and abilities. Kafka worked for an insurance company for most of his life, until tuberculosis forced him to retire, and therefore experienced routine and monotony. He never wanted any of his writing published but struggled with the dual identity of being an insurance worker and a writer.

The ideas of alienation and being an outsider, the futility and monotony of work, the struggle to be heard and understood are all areas from Kafka's life that impact directly on the story and the adapted play.

Berkoff

Steven Berkoff was born in London in 1937 but his parents were Russian-Jewish immigrants. His early life was fairly nomadic since his parents moved to different locations around London and also had a short spell in New York, all before he was 15. He felt lonely and isolated as a boy and his many moves prevented him from establishing friendships. His relationship with his father was strained and his father found it difficult to show any emotional connection with his son. After leaving school Berkoff went through a series of jobs such as selling biros, office clerk, messenger boy and an assistant in a clothing shop. It was while working as a clothing salesman in Germany that he first came across a copy of Kafka's *Metamorphosis* (*Die Verwandlung*). Berkoff's own childhood and the conflicts he faced are similar in many respects to Kafka's own dilemmas and it is easy to see how Berkoff found an empathy with the content and themes of the original text.

Think about...

Consider the similarities between Berkoff's upbringing and those of Kafka and the character Gregor.

Berkoff is an unusual writer in that he is also a director and an actor. His journey into writing plays was inspired by the fact that he found it hard to get parts in plays after graduating. He was also disillusioned with the theatre establishment and the way in which plays were written and cast. He found himself discontented with the bourgeois nature of theatre in Britain, and the style of acting and form of play writing.

Further reading

Try Berkoff's *Overview* (Faber 1994) and *Meditations on Metamorphosis* (Faber 1995).

Style

Berkoff has created a unique theatrical way of working with words and images. The language that he uses in his plays is very poetic and graphic in terms of its imagery. It has roots in his upbringing in London, and the rhythm and rhyme that regional slang can create, as well as a more literary reference with a Shakespearean quality at times, especially when dealing with universal themes such as love and death. The physical demands of Berkoff's plays, which are very evident in *Metamorphosis*, reveal the influence of European theatre and particularly Antonin Artaud, for whom creating meaning through image and movement was more important than the spoken word.

For more on Artaud, see pages 24–32.

Critical response

Berkoff has not always met with critical acclaim in Britain. His work is highly praised in continental Europe but has received a much less enthusiastic critical response in his home country. This may be because in many respects he fought against the British theatre establishment. His ideas never really fitted in with the kitchen-sink drama, the agit-prop theatre, or the commercial shows of the 1960s and 1970s. He is still seen as the 'enfant terrible' of British theatre and his work is often labelled as indulgent, controversial and over-stylised. His recent pieces *Requiem for Ground Zero* about the 9/11 tragedy, and his rewriting of the final days of Jesus in *Messiah* are testimony to his unique approach to plays and his mixed critical acclaim.

 Try to find out about the other movements in British theatre in the 1960s and 1970s, especially kitchen-sink drama and agit-prop theatre, and consider how different this was to Berkoff's work in style and content. Try to find some recent reviews of Berkoff's productions to see how they were received.

Plot and sub-plot

Metamorphosis is set in mid-Europe, probably just before the first world war. The story concerns the Samsa family: Father – a large and robust man; Mother – a loving but pained woman; Greta – the daughter, a sensitive spirit who was hoping to become a violinist; and Gregor – a travelling fabric salesman. The story quickly turns into a nightmare when Gregor wakes up one morning to find that he has turned into a large beetle. The play is then divided into two views of what happens next: we see and hear how the members of the family try to deal with this problem and Gregor talks directly to the audience to tell of his dilemma. For ease of understanding, you may wish to divide these two views into plot and sub-plot.

Although the metamorphosis of the title refers most obviously to the transformation of Gregor into an insect, by the end of the play each member of the family has undergone their own transformation. No longer able to live off Gregor's wages, the family discuss getting jobs themselves. Father is once again the man of the family, the object of his wife and daughter's respect and love. Greta grows as she assumes responsibility for her brother's care and all three remaining members of the family remark at the end on her blossoming into womanhood. Though Gregor gains clarity in his mind about his family's attitude to him, physically he deteriorates, especially after he is injured by his father.

Berkoff decided to use physical representation to show the beetle's transformation. This allows the actor playing Gregor to slip easily into human form when needed for flashback scenes and to communicate with the audience. This makes it easier to tell the story and begins to communicate that the story and its message are more significant than the characters themselves.

 Divide the play up into units – you should try to create between 15 and 20 units. Give each unit a title that sums up the action of that unit.

Working in groups of between four and six, try to represent the action of each unit as a freeze or still picture. What is happening in the unit? What are the characters thinking and feeling? What are you trying to communicate through the freeze? Use movement to link the freezes together and think about how movement can also

Further study

Try to read some of Berkoff's other plays and see if you can find similarities with *Metamorphosis* or identify any of the issues discussed in this section. His *The Trial* has a similar origin to *Metamorphosis*, as it was also originally a novel by Kafka.

Web link

www.iainfisher.com/berkoff.html is a comprehensive website with a useful photographic gallery, information on Berkoff and his plays and some really clear research papers on his life and work.

www.stevenberkoff.com is Berkoff's own website, and carries photographs and information about his plays.

For example, the first two units could be: Introduction to the family through gesture and Gregor's dilemma; Gregor comes home from a hard day and goes to bed.

create meaning. Try using music to accompany the realisation of the units. Establishing what you think are the important moments of the play will help you to come to terms with the plot.

For more on Brecht and his devices, see pages 17–24.

Think about how Brechtian devices such as alienation, third person and representation allow the importance of the story to be communicated. Try answering the following questions:

1. Define the following words: parable, analogy, allegory, metaphor. Which term would best describe the plot of *Metamorphosis*?

2. Who tells the story? What relationship does this build between character and audience, and what response does this create from the audience?

3. Consider the notions of: routine and futility; relationships and parasites; greed and ambition; heroism and adversity.

4. What is the chronology of the story, and how are events revealed?

Further study

Try finding a CD that would work effectively with the style and action of *Metamorphosis*. For example, try listening to the soundtracks to the films *Evil Dead*, *Edward Scissorhands* and *Beetlejuice*.

Write down what your units are, and try to represent each unit with an illustration. Describe what is important about each unit of the play.

Use of language

Even though *Metamorphosis* is layered and driven by physical work, words and dialogue are still important. The characters are very much represented as caricatures, yet they also have moments of revelation where the audience witnesses their personal journeys within the play. The language the family uses can be divided into four distinct areas:

➤ Direct address to the audience, explaining exactly what they are thinking and feeling. Gregor frequently tells the audience his thoughts, since he has no one else to speak to.

This is a device in the style of Brecht's alienation technique, which requires the audience to think about the situation and events of the play (see page 20). When the characters take on the role of narrator, their words are often a direct translation of Kafka's original story.

➤ Speaking in third person. Again, this is addressed to the audience, but the characters take the role of narrator, which allows us to understand that they are telling a story and it is this story that is important.

➤ Naturalistic dialogue. The characters talk to each other in a manner that allows us to believe they represent a real family and real people.

➤ Stylised and rhythmic language. This device is often used to support a theme or mood.

Gregor's language

The various uses of language that Gregor is given within the text show the complexity of the types of language that pervade *Metamorphosis*. He is able to talk to the audience as part of the narrative form of the piece, allowing the audience to think about his character and his predicament. Gregor is also able to talk to himself through soliloquy. In a sense, this allows him to be the universal representative of a human being, a sort of 'everyman' figure. Finally, Gregor talks to the family, although here, while the audience can generally hear him quite clearly, the family apparently can hear only grotesque sounds and noises characteristic of a beetle. By the end, the family refer to 'it' rather than 'him' or 'Gregor'.

The use of rhythm and repetition is very much part of the language format of the play and is usually accompanied by a physical realisation described by stage directions. This rhythmic and repetitive use of language not only communicates meaning through the words, but it also conveys this sense through the delivery of the words. This style of delivery supports and reveals the themes of monotony and routine and creates a ritual that is a very important part of the Samsas' life. Consider the scene in which the Samsa family realises that Gregor needs stale and rotten food now that he is a beetle, and begin to gather together all the old scraps they can find. The language pattern changes here and we begin to get a glimpse of a rhythmic list accompanied by a physical depiction of the food being collected.

Movement and images underpin all of the verbal work – just by flicking through the text you will come across many stage directions that indicate this. Through his instructions, Berkoff allows you to conjure up images and actions that should accompany, support and lead the words.

Not all the language used in the play is concerned with words. The stage directions often refer to the sounds of the play, such as knocking, tapping, ticking, banging or even the implied sound when the family are listening to Gregor's movements in his bedroom. Consider how meaning and mood can be communicated through such a soundscape.

Reread the play from the episode title 'Next Scene – Evening' up to and including Gregor's speech 'Oh I could weep with joy and satisfaction…'. In groups of between four and six, try using the acoustic of your fingers against a door, or a table turned on its end to represent a door, to create the following:

➢ The sound of a large insect running on the floor

➢ The sound of a large insect eating

➢ The sound of a large insect running up the wall and across the ceiling

➢ The sound of a large insect dropping from the ceiling and scuttling off.

Then, using naturalistic dialogue, consider how the Samsa family might respond to these noises. Try to show:

➢ Mrs Samsa is worried

➢ Greta doesn't want to upset Gregor

➢ Mr Samsa is too scared to do anything himself.

How important are sounds in the play? What does the family hear? How do they feel? How do you show what they feel? How much of the text is spoken word and how much is stage direction? How important is the language of imagery and sound within the play?

Rhythm, movement and image

Think about…

Give examples of the following types of language within this unit, stating who uses it and why:

✦ Direct address to the audience

✦ Internal monologue

✦ Naturalistic dialogue

✦ Ritualistic dialogue

✦ Rhythm/repetition in dialogue.

Metamorphosis is not just about dialogue but also the holistic nature of theatre and the power of visual theatre.

Sound-scaping

Practical exercise

Also try doing these in the dark – what effect does this have?

A good way to understand the events and action of the story is to draw a line after each episode/unit on your script. Units can often be distinguished by the use of blackout.

The structure of the story shows many of the elements of epic theatre (see page 19). In your exploration notes about form and structure, you need to discuss the Brechtian device of performance storytelling that allows us to realise that the actors are representing characters. The audience is required to make imaginative links with the action rather than just accept the action as real.

The beetle

Kafka is very vague about the form of the beetle in the original German, using a word meaning 'vermin', rather than a specific term meaning dung beetle or cockroach, as translations often do. His language is designed more to stress the monstrous, gross, but helpless and slightly ridiculous nature of the insect that Gregor has become.

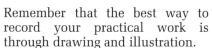

Tip

Remember that the best way to record your practical work is through drawing and illustration.

Further study

Which theatre practitioners would be best suited for this style of acting? Define the words poetic, symbolic, surreal and metaphorical.

Use matchstick people to represent the images created, and then comment on the importance of image work within the text.

Form and structure

The structure of *Metamorphosis* is episodic, meaning that the plot is created through episodes. An episode (or unit) could be:

➤ An episode that already exists within the play that has been titled by Berkoff, for example Scene 1 or 'Gregor's Dream'.

➤ An episode that exists as a flashback, for example the flashback to Christmas and the idea of sending Greta to the Conservatorium.

➤ An episode that describes an event or action within the story, for example the arrival and subsequent departure of the chief clerk.

As the plot is revealed episodically, storytelling relies on the imagination of the audience and their ability to create meaning and significance from the action by themselves. The different forms of speech discussed above are important in breaking down the play's structure, so that the characters not only talk to each other in dialogue, but also speak directly to the audience and narrate elements of the story.

The transformation of Gregor into a beetle is the pivotal action of the play and the catalyst that allows the audience to see the changes in the other characters. How this transformation is achieved theatrically is vital to the success of the play. The play is not a literal story and does not demand that we literally see Gregor changed into a beetle. This would be far too easy for the audience. They must imagine his grossness and feel the family's disgust. Therefore Berkoff chose to represent the beetle physically through the actor's use of voice, body and space. This also allows the actor playing the beetle to slip easily into human form when he needs to be in a flashback or to communicate with the audience.

Lie face down on the floor. Now pull your knees up and cross your arms in front of your face so that you are resting on your forearms, knees and shins. Through this simple and yet physically demanding position, Berkoff was able to mimic the legs, head and thorax of the beetle. His fingers, arms, head, upper body and legs could all work in isolation and begin to emulate the movement and manner of an insect. Move your head mechanically and in a jerky fashion. Push your arms forward and drag your body forward, supported by your knees. Try to create a continuous movement with this action. Berkoff also found that by swapping his crossed arms and having them on the correct side of his body, but forcing his elbows up by pushing his shoulders down, he could find another dynamic that enabled him to 'ooze' as well as crawl. Experiment with this physicality – you may find it incredibly hard and tiring. Look at Berkoff's introduction to the play to see his recommendations for physicalising the beetle and try to follow his instructions.

Metamorphosis is superficially about a young man who turns into a beetle. Describe the theatrical problems you encountered with this, and how you attempted to solve these problems. Think about the following:

➤ How are the characters first introduced? How is the beetle first introduced?

➤ What is the style of the storytelling?

➤ Draw freezes that could be acted for the arrival of the chief clerk section.

Visual, aural and spatial elements

Berkoff gives incredible detail about his vision for the set of the play. The text begins with a detailed page on the requirements of a skeletal framework of steel scaffolding. This fulfils many of the functional and symbolic requirements of the play, in that it represents an abstract sculpture of a giant insect, it solves the problem of the split space needed, and it even suggests the use of stools for family functions. Stage instructions in the text are layered. Berkoff often sets out the physical action of the episode, then the dialogue, and then the image that is required. These are not sequential instructions, rather generally simultaneous instructions that need to be layered together to complete the action of the scene.

Function refers to those elements that have to be in the design because the stage instructions (or the play) demand them. Symbol is the way in which the functional elements are designed, or the extra things that the designer brings to the play in order to create meaning or to emphasise themes. In *Metamorphosis* there has to be, for example, a living space for the family; an area that suggests Gregor's bedroom; a division between the two living spaces; some suggestion of location and time; some simple props to allow simple family functions such as the meal to happen. However, the set itself needs to represent and suggest elements of the deeper meaning, themes and moods of the play. These are:

➤ Surrealism and the dream-like/nightmarish quality of the story

➤ Insects and all the repellent and repulsive feelings that come with them

➤ Routine, monotony and futility

➤ The passing of time.

Lighting is very important in communicating the action to the audience. In its most raw element, it allows the action of the play and the characters to be seen by the audience. For example, the use of lighting could distinguish between the living area and Gregor's room; sharply focused light could create isolation for the person in that beam; cross fading of light or black-out can indicate the passing of time or the end of an episode; the speed of the appearance of light can startle, shock or have other effects on the audience.

Stark and snapped white light contrasting with black-outs are a major feature of the stage directions. The monochromatic set may enforce the idea of a dream or even match the colouring of a beetle.

Stage directions

Web link

The following website shows Mark Cavalier's set designs for the 1989 Cloud Nine Productions interpretation of *Metamorphosis*: www.shef.ac.uk/english/literature/lighting/designprocess.htm.

Function and symbol

Lighting

Consider how the use of colours in lighting can create symbolic meanings. Red, for example, can mean anger, rage, madness etc.

Go through the play text and write down a lighting plot purely based on the stage directions. Use the following chart to help with format:

Lighting effect	Action	Reason
Light backcloth	Family enter	Creates silhouettes. Physical representation of characters important
Front light comes up	Revealing family	Moving from surreal to real
Lights snap on	Revealing Gregor as normal	Scenes of pre-insect light
etc.		

Costume

The costumes in *Metamorphosis* need to:

➢ Allow the actors to move and work very physically

➢ Indicate a class status

➢ Indicate a location

➢ Indicate a period

➢ Allow the actor playing Gregor to slip between being a human and a beetle with ease

➢ Indicate the notions of surrealism

➢ Emphasise the monochrome nature of the play.

Sound and music

Sound and music are an important part of the layering of *Metamorphosis* and can have the following functions within the play:

➢ Support or lead movement or ballet sequence

➢ Underscore a monologue or dialogue to enhance mood

➢ Link scenes to show the passing of time

➢ Indicate flashback or flash forward

➢ Create a mood.

Staging

The play demands a certain style of staging as we have discovered from our previous exploration of form, structure and plot. This style is best achieved through allowing the actors to create with their own bodies what they need physically and through relying on the imagination of the audience rather than on a complex set. In Berkoff's opening address on stage setting at the front of the text he clearly states: 'The stage is void of all props – everything is mimed – apart from three black stools.' The actors are required to use their voices, bodies and the space available to create the world that the characters exist in.

Berkoff will generally not allow chairs into his rehearsal space because it allows the actor to relax mentally and physically, instead of becoming fully aware of and engaged with the space they are working in.

Further study

When working on the staging elements, try to consider the following words and phrases: stylised, grotesque, use of image, choreographed movement, ballet, total theatre, physical theatre, theatre of cruelty, surreal, clockwork, ritual.

 Imagine that you are the set designer for a production of *Metamorphosis*. How do you think the set should look? Consider:

➢ The function of the space – what must be there

➢ The symbolism you could use – what the space could look like

> Those stage directions within the text that demand a specific look.

Draw the set as you feel the demand. Then try to draw an alternative set, but incorporate your conclusions about function and symbol.

Vinegar Tom

Vinegar Tom is a play written in 1976 by Caryl Churchill about a small community in England in the 17th century.

Contextualising the play

Churchill was born in London in 1938. She studied English at Oxford University where she began to write plays. After graduating she began her career writing for BBC radio. Writing for radio was instrumental in developing her own unique writing style. Two specific areas of development were:

1. As the spoken word is the chief form of communication in a radio play, the words had to have a real value and significance because:

   ◆ The plot was carried by the words

   ◆ The characters were only formed by the words they spoke

   ◆ The form and structure were created by how the words were used, since what was spoken as text – and was also created through silence and ambiguity as subtext – became an essential part of her style.

2. Writing for the radio liberated rather than restricted her. She was free from the necessity to write stage directions and to think about the visual aspect of the plays. This freedom allowed her to experiment with:

   ◆ The structure of the play and the length of scenes

   ◆ Plot, the chronology of scenes and the ability to move quickly in time

   ◆ Location and the ability to jump quickly from place to place.

[?] Consider the difference between a radio play and a play written for the theatre. What impact would writing for such different audiences have on stage directions, location indicators, movement instructions, and set descriptors? Try to find an example of two different types of play by Churchill to make this comparison.

From 1974 to 1975 Churchill was the resident dramatist at the Royal Court Theatre in London, a theatre that is well known for encouraging new and radical writing. This position allowed Churchill to begin writing specifically for the theatre.

During this time she started collaborations with theatre companies, most famously with Joint Stock and Monstrous Regiment, which were companies dedicated to looking at feminist issues. These

Further study

Try to find out the titles of Churchill's early radio works and write a brief sentence to sum up what each one is about.

" This was a new way of working. I felt briefly shy and daunted, wondering if I would be acceptable, then happy and stimulated by the discovery of shared ideas and the enormous energy and feeling of possibilities in the still new company. "

Churchill in the introduction to *Vinegar Tom* (Methuen 1985)

Further study

Try to find out how Churchill created the play *Mad Forest* through workshop collaboration. Find a copy of *The Skriker* and consider how this play was written using a new theatrical structure to tell the story.

Vinegar Tom and The Crucible

" I wanted to write a play about witches with no witches in it: a play not about evil, hysteria and possession by the devil but about poverty, humiliation and prejudice and how women accused of witchcraft saw themselves. "

Churchill (introduction to *Vinegar Tom)*

Web link

A good website for research into Caryl Churchill, *Vinegar Tom* and witchcraft can be found at the University of Puget Sound: http://library.ups.edu/instruct/ricig/vtom.htm.

collaborations had enormous impact on the way Churchill wrote plays. Moving away from writing in isolation, she found the whole process of meeting, thinking, sharing, working with actors and then writing incredibly exciting.

This collaborative approach to writing supports the character creation so important to the drive of Churchill's plays. The attention to detail in the language used, the feeling of a real history and life for the characters, the emotional depth and poignancy that each character has, have all been the product of being able to work directly with actors. The character is not a fiction created on paper but a tangible person that is formed in collaboration with an actor. It was during this time and this phase of her work that *Vinegar Tom* was written with Monstrous Regiment.

Like its better-known American counterpart, *The Crucible* by Arthur Miller, *Vinegar Tom* would appear to be about witches and witchhunts. Yet is a story that represents and examines much more than this.

The two main things that separate *Vinegar Tom* from *The Crucible* are:

➤ *The Crucible*'s characters and events are rooted in the historical witchhunts of Salem, Massachusetts in 17th-century America. *Vinegar Tom* is not based on precise historical fact or detail. It is much more loosely set and was inspired by the fact that Monstrous Regiment theatre company wanted to perform a play about witches and the Joint Stock theatre company wanted to do a play about social reform and the position of women in the 17th century. While writing *Vinegar Tom*, Churchill also wrote *Light Shining in Buckinghamshire* for Joint Stock.

➤ *The Crucible* is very much concerned with the events of the past even though there are resonances of the McCarthy political anti-communist witchhunts of the early 1950s that were occurring in the USA when the play was written. *Vinegar Tom* plays with time – the songs within the play are a modern commentary on the action, which is set in the past. Churchill wanted these songs delivered by the actors in modern dress and not as the characters of the play. This forces the audience to be aware of the modern implications of past events. It links the action of the past to the attitudes of the present. The portrayal and treatment of women is focal to the play and this is brought into a modern relevance by the songs and the way they are delivered.

Despite the fact that witches are a key starting point for *Vinegar Tom*, in the end it is not a play about witches but a play about why women were accused of witchcraft – about how the accusation of witchcraft was a scapegoat for women who were old, poor, single or sexually unconventional.

 Try to watch the film version of *The Crucible* with Daniel Day Lewis. In the play text the actual events of the witchcraft are left very ambiguous and may or may not have happened. How are they depicted in the film and how are you left feeling about what happened and the people involved? Try specifically to consider the treatment of women in that community.

Plot and sub-plot

Vinegar Tom is named after a cat owned by an old woman in the play who comes to be accused of witchcraft. It is set in a small community in 17th-century England and concerns the lives of a small group of women from various social backgrounds over the course of a short period of time.

It is a play about people and not so much about action or events. The story is not comprised of a plot and a sub-plot as such, but rather a series of parallel plots surrounding the small group of characters involved. Each character in the story is as important as another. There is a real sense of ensemble in the playing of the story and also of each character's worth to the meaning of the story. Although each of the characters has their own journey within the play, many of the characters overlap and are a part of one another's stories.

Integrated into the story of the women is a commentary of songs that are required to be sung out of character in order to create a modern reference to the period action. The songs are not necessarily a direct comment on the scene that has happened or is about to happen but are more concerned with alerting the audience to the relevance of various attitudes towards women.

The story is also given an epilogue in which two historical figures are represented as a music-hall act and perform extracts from the once-credited handbook on the identification and treatment of witches called *Malleus Maleficarum* ('The Hammer of Witches').

Who am I? Where am I? What do I want?

In groups of three or four, take each of the scenes in the play and create a one-line statement concerning:

➤ The character you are playing

➤ The location of the scene

➤ What you want to achieve in this scene.

Each of these statements should be presented with a physical gesture or in a freeze. For example in Scene 1, two members of the group should represent the Man and Alice.

Man:

➤ I am a man, my name is unimportant because I am representing men and their lusts and the casual way in which they use women for sex

➤ I am in some bushes near the roadside because it is convenient to have sex

➤ I want to be powerful and I use sex to feel powerful.

Alice:

➤ I am Alice and I am in my twenties

➤ I am in a field because it is romantic

➤ I want love and I want to get away from my home village.

This exercise not only deals with the chronology of events and the location but begins to show how the plot is driven by the revelation of who the characters are and what they want.

Further study

There is a dark significance to the title chosen by Churchill, as 'Vinegar Tom' was also the name given to a type of contraceptive used after sex. Raw honey and organic apple vinegar would have been used and applied using a sponge. Try to find out about 'Vinegar Tom' or 'Cat's Claw Extract'.

Web link

For more on this work, visit www.malleusmaleficarum.org.

This technique is linked to the concepts of given circumstances, units, objectives and superobjectives put forward by Stanislavski (see page 12).

Chart each of the 21 scenes. Next to the scene number describe the location and the characters that are in it, and note a sentence that sums up the scene or the song. For example:

Scene 2: Jack and Margery's

➢ They are married and are farmers in their forties

➢ They talk about how they want to expand their farm

➢ Betty, the landowner's daughter, visits

➢ There is a sense of social hierarchy.

You could then chart the journey of each of the characters throughout the play. This will help you to understand the importance of the parallel plots in *Vinegar Tom*.

Use of language

The language spoken by the characters is an important tool in playwriting for Churchill. *Vinegar Tom* is an excellent example of a play in which the foremost method of communication to the audience is the words the characters speak, the style in which they speak and the way in which lyrics are used by an out-of-role chorus. A variety of forms of language are fused together in *Vinegar Tom*.

Naturalistic dialogue

The credibility of Churchill's writing in *Vinegar Tom* comes from the believability of her characters. The way they are created allows the audience to accept that they could be real and that they could exist outside the play. The choice of words, rhythms and the way the words are placed in relation to each other creates a dialect, a social class and a life that we as the audience can accept. The heart of this language can be seen in the ease with which characters communicate in their everyday, naturalistic exchanges.

This is particularly evident in Scene 8 when Alice and Susan visit Ellen, the Cunning Woman. By using short phrases juxtaposed against the longer responses of the Cunning Woman, Churchill quickly gives us a sense of place and time but also of character, status and self-doubt. What is also very important to the success of her everyday text is the complexity of what the character wants and the subtext that exists beneath the words.

In groups of three, improvise a visit to the Cunning Woman. For each of the characters decide what will be spoken and what will be the subtext of the conversation. This can be done by deciding what you really want to say but dare not.

Consider how you create everyday language and how you transcribe a dialect through words. What can subtext bring to a language? Think about how words can mean one thing on the surface but can have a greater significance underneath the surface.

Ritualistic repartee

Churchill uses religious and sexual imagery with ease, as if it is part of everyday language. She is able to create a repartee between characters that is full of wit and wicked humour, and that refers to other, darker things. Often what is said is not what is meant and there is often a rich subtext. This is extremely clear in Scene 1 between the Man and Alice. They have just had sex and they tease each other with questions and promises. The language in this scene sets the tone for the play and moves between agreement and argument, wit and worry, and light and dark.

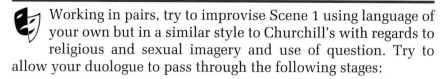

Working in pairs, try to improvise Scene 1 using language of your own but in a similar style to Churchill's with regards to religious and sexual imagery and use of question. Try to allow your duologue to pass through the following stages:

➤ A desire to be friends
➤ Sharing what you dream of being
➤ One of you wants commitment – one of you doesn't
➤ A breakdown and a conflict between you.

How does your language change and differ?

Churchill shifts the mood of the play very quickly by changing the style of language. Moving from an emotional scene of interrogation, denial, confession and betrayal in Scene 14 to a very matter-of-fact direct-address monologue delivered by the Witchfinder's assistant to the audience in Scene 15, creates an unsettling effect for the audience. The audience may become unsure of their own feelings and empathies, which in turn can create alienation in the way that Brecht enjoyed playing with his audiences.

Consider a scenario similar to Scene 14 of *Vinegar Tom* in which the perpetrator of the violence or crime explains that they are only doing their job. You could use one of the following scenarios: a torturer in a current extremist regime where prisoners are political; a guard in a concentration camp in the second world war; a doctor carrying out shock treatment on patients who are considered insane. Improvise a direct-address monologue in which you are the perpetrator of the violence, but make it a dispassionate description of the job. How does this make you feel as an actor and/or as the character? How does the style of this speech affect your audience?

Churchill uses song to commentate on the action of the previous scene and also to create modern relevance for the action of the play. She emphasises that the *actors*, not the characters, should sing each song. She instructs the cast to deliver the songs in modern dress so that the audience can separate the characters and the action of the play from the song and the message of the song. This creates a distance from the action and alienates the audience in the sense that they have to review and rethink what they are seeing and what they think the play is saying.

What difference would it make to the play if the characters, not the actors, sang the songs? Think about other plays with songs, such as *Blood Brothers*, in which the characters sing the songs in role. What effect does that have on them and on the audience's relationship with them?

Direct address

For more on Brecht's ideas on alienation, see pages 17–24.

Further reading

Death and the Maiden by Ariel Dorfman (Nick Hern Books 1996) examines the relationship between torturer and victim. *The Investigation* by Peter Weiss (Marion Boyars 1982) is a dramatic re-creation of evidence given in a war trial concerning Auschwitz. *A Mother's Voice* by Chris Owen (Hodder Arnold 2000) is set in a mythical central American country, and deals with the disappearance of innocent people.

Third-person commentary

Read Scene 13 and write a song that picks up the idea of Alice making Jack impotent. This song could be an ironic comment about how it is a woman's fault that men get turned on by the way they dress, behave and allow themselves to be models in magazines and on TV. You could call it: 'You're nothing but a tease.'

Try to perform this song after you have read or performed Scene 13. Remember to separate the characters in the scene from those singing the song, perhaps by using different people or by removing a token costume used as the character. Consider:

➢ How you felt delivering the song as an actor

➢ The effect of the song on the audience.

Satirical comedy patter

In Scene 21, Churchill creates a comedy routine with the characters Sprenger and Kramer in order to satirise the serious handbook that these men wrote in the 17th century to identify and deal with witches. The dark comedy of this scene comes from the very thought that the words used and the characters represented were real. The ludicrous nature of their depiction and delivery heightens the fact that these words and people were taken seriously and once had a significant and fatal impact on their society.

Create a physical routine with the words of Scene 21. Try to imagine Reeves and Mortimer, French and Saunders, or Ant and Dec doing this routine – how would these duos approach the words? Give each line a gesture and create a routine that could be performed nightly as part of a music hall season. Try to find a soundtrack that you could use to represent the feeling of this scene.

Form and structure

Vinegar Tom is made up of a series of short episodes set in the past, occasionally punctuated with songs that are removed from the setting of the play and sung by the actors, not the characters. The final scene takes the form of an epilogue and is performed in a separate style by separate characters to form the story. The structure of the episodes is in chronological order but not in a consistent time relation, which means that two episodes may be separated by one minute but others by a day or a week.

The form that the episodes take is a series of dialogues with an occasional monologue. The story is driven by the characters that inhabit the world of the play. The story is stopped and reflected on through the use of song, designed to make the audience aware that they must not get too carried away with emotional content but must think about its relevance to use in the present.

There is potential for the creation of stylised and physical work within the text, for example, in Scene 6 where Betty is being bled by the Doctor. However, it must be noted that Churchill's intent was not to portray the Doctor as a sadistic man, but, more importantly, to show women being humiliated while men go about their work in a cold and efficient fashion.

In *Vinegar Tom*, Churchill uses the notion of role reversal to add impact to the characters and to the actions of the characters. Having women play male characters creates an agenda, making the audience aware that these are men and that their actions are in direct response to the fact that they are men. This can be seen especially in the final scene with Kramer and Sprenger.

 Read Scenes 8, 9, 10 and 11. All of these scenes take place at the Cunning Woman Ellen's cottage. In a very short period of actual play time we are confronted with three parallel plots with Ellen as the catalyst. There is no indication of the real time covered within the play but we can assume that there is some time between them, since 10 and 11 feature the same character, Jack, on a return visit. In a small group, place the person playing Ellen in the centre of your space. If your group is large enough, allocate people to play Alice, Susan, Betty, Jack and Margery. If your group is smaller, then the same people can play both Alice and Susan, Betty and Jack, and Margery. Get the groups to stand in separate corners of the space and then face Ellen. In turn, get Ellen to ask each of the groups 'What do you want of me?' Get each of the characters to initiate a dialogue or create a monologue in response.

List the different forms used in the telling of the story. Try to identify each form scene by scene, considering duologue, dialogue, monologue, direct address, potential for stylised work and song.

Visual, aural and spatial elements

Churchill gives minimal instructions as to the look and sound of the space within which the characters live. As Churchill's formative years were spent writing for the radio, this influenced the freedom with which she uses space and time, and the ease with which her characters move between these areas.

Churchill is constantly reminding us throughout the play that this is a piece of theatre. The songs and the finale of Kramer and Sprenger are reminders that this a story with a message and at times we need to distance ourselves from the emotional content of the play to form an opinion about it. This form and structure would sit comfortably in a more minimal and representational space and setting. The power of the play is in the words, and therefore it would be interesting to create a tokenistic set with the actors in charge of it. This would allow the actors to use the set to create a location and to come back to it as a theatre to sing the songs.

Go through each of the scenes and briefly note where the action of each scene happens. For example: Scene 1: Roadside; Scene 2: Jack and Margery's farm; Scene 3: Inside Joan's cottage. This will give you an overview of the settings for each of the scenes.

 Choose a key prop to represent each of the scenes. Try to use props that give an impression of the scene and signify an important part of either the location, the atmosphere or the content. For example, you could use an old candelabra or a candle for the scenes with the Cunning Woman. Not only would this give an impression of a small room or cottage but would be tremendous

Weblink

Look at the University of Denver's website (www.du.edu/thea/designs/Design-VinegarTom.html) to see an example of a naturalistic set that tries to communicate the areas that are real. Such a set draws the audience into the world of *Vinegar Tom* and supports the characters and the reality of the action of the play. It would also make the modern song commentary all the more of a contrast when it occurred.

in embellishing atmosphere and creating tension. A milk churn could represent the farm, an old wooden box could represent the poverty of Joan's house, a smart wooden chair could represent the decadence of the landowner's house. Choosing props as symbolic representations as well as functional tools is a good way of creating a meaningful and yet minimalistic set.

You could take your minimalist set one step further by choosing a way of presenting these props to the audience through metaphor. Drawing a pentagram on the floor and placing one key prop on each point of the five stars would immediately suggest to the audience that the play is about witchcraft. Setting up this suggestion would be an ideal starting point before breaking this misconception down with the message of the play.

Another way of creating location – and a change in location and time – is through lighting and sound effects. The short scenes and various locations as well as the draw back to modern time through song provide great potential for a lighting and sound plot. The whole play could be performed in an open space and could be led and supported just by lighting and sound effects.

Write down a suggested scene-by-scene lighting and sound plan that would indicate place and time. Think carefully about the type of light used, the colour and the angle of lighting. Consider what sound effects could be created acoustically and through recording to suggest place and time, to help with change of location and time and also to support atmosphere.

Vinegar Tom and much of Churchill's other writing has the same quality as Shakespeare, in that the location is fully realised in the dialogue – it is always clear where the characters are, when the action is taking place and why the characters are there. What should be clear from your work here is that the play fits easily and comfortably in a range of styles of visual, aural and spatial representation.

Text in Performance

What do I have to do?

The unit

Text in Performance is the most practical element of your AS course. To quote the examiners, in this unit you are expected to 'communicate ideas, feelings, and/or meaning to an audience in response to a scripted play'.

To achieve this you must:

➤ Take on the role of a performer or designer within a performance company

➤ Work collaboratively to rehearse and perform a play

➤ Communicate a clear interpretation of the play in performance

➤ Work with a director.

Essentially, therefore, you will be involved in the process of choosing, designing, rehearsing and performing a play. For many of you, this will be the most rewarding aspect of your AS course. It may also be the most difficult aspect.

 Log

You should keep a log of all the sessions that you are involved in and the work that you cover. This includes lessons, discussions, group rehearsals and performances you have seen that may be relevant to the play – or style of play – you are studying.

This log should cover:

➤ **What** you did during the sessions. This could be an account of the lesson, practical session, discussion.

➤ **How** you did the work. This should show the style of work you were involved in, and be communicated through notes, illustrations and diagrams showing the different parts of the lesson or sessions.

➤ **Why** you covered this material. This should explain the relevance of the work you have covered and explain the point of the exercises or types of work covered in relation to the text.

Try to write and draw these notes immediately after each session so that they are fresh in your mind. They are invaluable when it comes to creating the final Context Summary Notes for unit 3.

Assessment

This aspect of your course is assessed and marked by a visiting examiner, who will visit your centre for the performance of the play. Your teacher will also need to video the performance and send that video recording to the examiner after the production. This video ensures there is a record of your production so that if there are any problems or queries regarding your performance it can be used as a reference.

Criteria The examiner will assess you in three different areas:

1. The judgements you have made when **interpreting** your role within the production as a performer or designer.	You need to indicate that you understand the play text you have chosen. You need to show that you and your director (see page 82) have creatively and thoughtfully created a concept for the play as a whole. Your work as a character or as a designer needs to support this overall concept for the play.
2. Your **technical ability** as a performer or designer in applying this interpretation to the production.	As a performer, you need to show a strong command of vocal skills. This includes understanding and being able to use clarity, pace, pause, projection and inflection. You also need to demonstrate a strong command of movement in terms of characterisation, gesture, stillness and other physical skills. If you choose to work on the design of your production rather than perform, you need to demonstrate a high level of competence when using the relevant materials and equipment. Your designs for the production must be well-executed and indicate that you have really understood the physical demands of your play.
3. The way you **communicate** meaning to an audience as a performer or a designer.	This means remaining focused and engaged throughout your performance, whatever role you are in. It means being aware of how your role complements the others around you, and using appropriate reactions to the other performers on stage. If you are a designer, communication refers to making sure you understand how your design work contributes to the performance, and the effect it has on an audience: your work must enhance and complement the work of the actors, and have impact for the audience.

Dos and don'ts The exam board sets out some specific rules and regulations to consider in terms of this module, and while your teacher will be aware of them, it's worth your bearing them in mind:

➢ The play you choose for this unit must be different from the plays you have studied for the Exploration of Drama and Theatre unit.

➢ The play you choose must provide you with a sufficient challenge as a performer or designer. We will give you guidance on the choice and selection of plays later in this section.

See page 79.

➢ It is suggested that you should have between three and nine people in your cast. Up to three students can be designers.

➢ It is likely that your teacher will direct the play, although it is not unacceptable to have a student director.

➢ The play should run for between 30 and 60 minutes depending on how big your cast is. It is important that you all get a chance to demonstrate your skills, but the performance must not be over-long.

The purpose of this unit

This element of your course should not be seen in isolation. You should not think of it as the part of the exam in which you get to perform a play. This performance unit is very much a part of the progression of both your AS and A2 course, and you need to think carefully about how it fits into the exam as a whole.

Links with unit 1   You should have covered Exploration of Drama and Theatre before taking on Text in Performance. This first unit should have made you think about how plays are written and constructed, and how they can be interpreted. This process of thinking is called **deconstruction**: the process whereby you break a play down to see what it is made of, how it is made, what it is trying to say and why. Your study for this unit should have made you aware, therefore, of:

➤ How a play is told through plot and sub-plot

➤ How the story is communicated through different types of language

➤ How the story could be staged through form and structure

➤ How a play could look and sound through the way it is staged

➤ How the play can be made relevant to both performer and audience by an understanding of its context.

Your work on unit one should have made you aware of the different approaches you can have to staging plays. These are perhaps best considered through the work and ideas of major practitioners such as Stanislavski, Brecht and Artaud.

You should now also be aware of important elements in performance that must be dealt with when bringing a play from page to stage:

➤ The way you deal with the subject matter and the choices you have in dealing with it

➤ Different ways of exploring and interpreting characters

➤ Understanding and interpreting meaning

➤ Applying physical actions to text and blocking it

➤ Vocalising the text.

Your work on the Exploration of Drama and Theatre unit (as well as the information in the Understanding Theatre chapter of this guide) is there to help you when working on this performance aspect of the course. You must apply the skills and thinking processes gained in the early part of the course to this second unit: because of this early work, you should now be in a position to take a play text that you do not know and be able to deconstruct it with a mind to casting, rehearsing and performing it.

Choosing a play

At A2 you will be expected to devise your own performance piece; here you must work with a play script already in existence. The exam board does not prescribe which texts you should use: the choice is completely up to you. However, it does warn that the choice of text is crucial: it is vital that you pick a script that suits your group and that will inspire you all creatively. So where should you look for advice on choosing a play?

The exam board gives some excellent advice on how to choose and cast a play in their Coursework Guide, available at www.edexcel.org.uk. They also give a list of example play choices and a table of possible plays broken down by title, author and the number of male and female characters. This would be a good starting place when considering which play to do.

For a comprehensive look at these practitioners, see the Understanding Theatre chapter on pages 8–32.

Samuel French also publishes an excellent guide to selecting plays for performance, which is available from www.samuelfrench-london.co.uk. Samuel French has various classification lists within their publication, but in Section A they arrange titles according to number of characters and also by type of play.

Practical considerations

Of course, this very important decision may well have been taken already by your teacher. If that is the case, they will have already gone through the following thought processes, which, if the play is still to be chosen, you will need to consider.

Firstly there are some **practical** questions to think about:

1. How many students are in your group?

It is always a good idea to try to find a play that has a cast the same size as your group. It is also a good idea to try to find a play that has a sense of balance, in that the parts are of equal measure. This may not always be possible and there may be members of your group who actively seek smaller parts. However, you must remember that the examiner can only mark you when you are performing and that therefore everyone in your group must have time on stage and a role that challenges them and brings out the best in them.

There are many plays available that allow an equality of performance and also allow multi-role playing, whereby you or members of your group can play more than one role. This will be covered in the next section.

Sometimes a large class finds that they all want to do the same play rather than split into smaller groups to fulfil the regulations about group size. In this situation the exam board can be flexible, though remember that the size-constraint regulation is there to allow the examiner to concentrate on no more than nine students per performance – it is in your interests to be properly seen by the examiner marking your piece.

You must also remember that not only should the play and the part you play offer you the opportunity to be challenged and show your understanding as an actor or designer, but you must also be able to write about this experience for unit 3. Therefore you must choose a play that will allow you to enjoy, intellectualise and reflect on the process.

2. What sexes are the members of your group?

There is nothing in the exam rubric that states you cannot have girls playing boys or vice versa, and the examiners' report from last year notes that some interesting work was done in this area. However, the rubric encourages you to retain the artistic integrity of your chosen play and this may not always be best achieved by cross-gender casting. Think carefully before you take this decision and ask whether it suits or supports the intention of the play. You may of course choose to have a female Hamlet in order to make a theatrical point or statement but try to avoid making the decision out of a logistical necessity rather than an artistic concept.

Exam board

In this scenario your school should contact the examiners to let them know what you are doing. In order to allow yourself the potential for the maximum possible marks in this part of the exam it is always best to adhere to the rubric (instructions).

3.   How do we make a play fit the time restraints of the exam?
Whatever play you choose, it must meet the time restraints of the exam (as a rule, between 30 and 60 minutes depending on the size of your group, with larger groups nearer an hour). The exam board gives a formula of five minutes per candidate in the group as a basic rule. What is important is that you must have an opportunity to show a sense of development as an actor. This is probably best achieved by presenting the whole play or the essence of the whole play.

If you have chosen a play that is longer than an hour you could still show the essence of the play by:

➢ Selecting a continuous extract or a whole act or scene and representing missing moments or events from the play through abstract movement, narration, tableaux.

➢ Selecting aspects of one particular plot or strand of the play by choosing particular scenes that support this.

➢ Making careful cuts and edits that still allow a sense of the story and character development. The examiners have stated that candidates have done best when there was a sense that the entire play had been taught and explored and then creatively edited. Missing moments or events from the play could again be told or represented through abstract movement, narration and tableaux. This could easily be achieved with a text such as *Metamorphosis* (covered on pages 61–69 of this guide) in which that type of theatrical form is already heavily used, or could easily be used with a text such as *Macbeth* to represent action-driven parts of the story.

Remember that the time constraint is there as a help to you. A longer play will demand longer rehearsal time, more sustained focus and concentration during the performance and greater production demands around the play. These areas may impede you rather than help you.

Secondly there are some **artistic** questions to answer:

Artistic considerations

1.   What type of play do you want to choose?
It's very important that you choose a play that will lay down some artistic challenges and allow you to work at a level appropriate for the AS course. It is additionally important that you are able to write about the process of rehearsing and performing the play for your Text in Context work (unit 3).

For unit 3, the chosen play needs to allow you to consider:

➢ The characters that populate it

➢ How to tell the story of the play using theatrical ideas

➢ How you can bring an interpretation to the text

➢ The intent of the playwright and the relevance for your audience.

Reflect on the work you've already done for unit 1 and what you know of the key theatre practitioners. Use your interests as developed here to help you decide on a text. Consider the following questions:

➢ Have you been interested by a particular style of approach to the content of a play?
For example: epic theatre and storytelling techniques as discovered in your work on Brecht.

➢ Have you been challenged or engaged by a particular theme or issue?
For example: witchcraft and the supernatural as explored in Vinegar Tom.

➢ Have you been excited by a particular approach to rehearsal and the realisation of characters?
For example: emotional truth and the work of Stanislavski.

➢ Have you been inspired by a specific style of performance?
For example: the Theatre of Cruelty and the work of Artaud.

➢ Have you been engaged by a particular period of theatre history?
For example: ancient Greek drama.

➢ Have you considered your target audience and what may be most relevant for them?
For example: an issue-based piece relating to young people.

Try to find plays that lend themselves to the passions and interests that have been stirred by the work you have done so far.

2.   How do you choose roles within the group?

Choosing roles and casting the parts in your chosen play can be rather problematic at times, and a cause of tension and stress within the group. This is a tension and stress that a group can do without at a time when group work and shared motivation is all-important to the success of the project. Be sensitive and prepared to compromise, and try to balance your own personal preferences with an awareness of what will be best for the production as a whole.

Obviously, the first decision you need to make is whether you wish to be a performer or designer. It is unlikely that you or a fellow student would be asked to direct, as it is expected that your teacher should direct this element of your course. If you have a desire to direct then bear in mind that this will be available as a possibility in the devising unit of the A2 course, in which student directing is encouraged.

Being a designer

If you choose to take on the role of designer for your group, you will need to decide whether you want to focus on one of the nominated skills or a combination of more than one element. The choices are: lighting, setting/props, costume, masks and sound.

The role of designer in any of these areas is very much concerned with the journey of exploration, interpretation and realisation of the play. You would be expected to make a full and important contribution to all areas of rehearsal as well as the final performance.

The decision to take on a design role should be a positive one, based on a real enthusiasm and desire to explore the selected area. It should not be a default decision arrived at because you don't

Web link

The different design skills have different criteria for assessment. A very comprehensive and clear grid of requirements is available from the exam board at www.edexcel.org.uk.

want to perform, don't like the play or don't like the characters in the play.

It is in many ways a more difficult role than performing, because you need to approach the tasks in a really structured and self-disciplined fashion. You will be required to attend all rehearsals and contribute actively in these sessions, as well as working alone to build up knowledge and understanding of your chosen skill before implementing it.

Having said all that, acting as the designer can be incredibly rewarding in terms of artistic satisfaction, and can be an excellent way of securing good marks in this unit. Not only will you be judged by your contribution to the final performance, but you will also have an opportunity to give a short presentation to the examiner after the performance, outlining your thinking and the processes by which you made decisions.

Casting

For those who have made the decision to perform, the process of casting the play can be critical to its success as well as to the harmony and work ethic of the group. Of course, this may be solved by your teacher making casting decisions, but even so, they will probably go through some clear thought processes before arriving at decisions.

Don't be frightened of holding auditions among your group to see if anyone finds an immediate or natural affinity with any of the parts through reading them aloud or learning a short extract. Perform these pieces in front of each other so that there is a democracy and a sense of sharing from the beginning. Talk openly but positively about the auditions but see if any majority opinions emerge. Take some time to workshop the play and give everybody an opportunity to play many different roles from the play. What you may think at first is the dream role for you may turn out not to be after a chance to improvise around it or represent it in a more informal session outside of a rehearsal.

Try to play to the strengths of the group and don't be frightened of letting more experienced members of your group take on the more difficult roles. Big parts don't automatically mean big marks. What counts is the success of the whole play and your role within that success. The size of your role is unimportant as long as it contributes to a successful whole.

Create an ensemble focus for the play by keeping your cast in full view of the audience at all times, and allow the mechanism of theatre to be in view of the audience. Costume changing, set preparation, playing more than one role – all can be presented to the audience in a way that is just as important as the events, the characters and the words they speak. This is a great way of giving equal importance to all members of the cast.

Choose a play that is by its very nature an ensemble play, in which the cast is required to play many parts, or a play that affords the potential to share the lead role in a clear and coherent way. Or choose a play in which the characters are unimportant and may

A more specific brief for the designer can be found later in this chapter in the sections on the plays we have chosen to look at. See pages 87–112.

> " There are no small parts, only small actors. "
> Motto of Stanislavski's Moscow Art Theatre

appear as numbers rather than names, but the story is all-important. If you are confused about what types of play these could be or want some examples, don't worry, because this section will go on to give you tangible texts to work with.

Rehearsing

Organisation is a very important key to success in this unit. The two plays that are given as example texts later in this section will give you some clear ideas as to how to approach rehearsals in particular but there are some general principles that need to be recognised.

Schedule   Try to create a rehearsal schedule. It should be recognised and understood that, although all your lessons during this unit of study may be given up to rehearsal, you will be expected to rehearse outside lesson time as well. Break the play down into manageable sections or units of action that could be rehearsed within the time limit of your lesson or in the time allocated outside of the lesson.

The exam board gives an excellent pair of equations for the relationship between text and rehearsal, and between rehearsal and performance. They suggest that:

1 page of text = 2 minutes of performance time

1 minute of performance time = 1 hour of rehearsal

These are good general principles to use when breaking down the play into sections that could be rehearsed in your lessons and sessions.

When creating a rehearsal schedule, put down the day and date of all the slots available to you leading up to the performance date. It is sometimes useful to work backwards in the schedule by placing the performance date, the dress rehearsal, the technical rehearsal and the full run first, in order to ensure that you give space and importance to these rehearsals. Then start from the beginning date and enter in the selected sections of your play, in chronological order. Be sure to leave slots for repetition of rehearsed sections and an opportunity to run sections together as you get closer to the full run.

It is also a good idea to have a column indicating the specific characters needed at that rehearsal. Here's an example:

Day and date	Lesson or time	Scene/section to be rehearsed	Who is needed
Monday 1 March	Periods one and two	Devise the opening sequence	Everyone

Try to set yourself clear targets for each rehearsal. They may be as simple as 'We must block three pages of text in order to create the staging patterns for those scenes'. They may refer to exploring and understanding a character, a theme or a passage of dialogue. They may even be as practical as working out entrances or exits for people or props. Try to declare the target for each rehearsal at the beginning and reflect on whether or not it has been achieved at the end.

✎ Give yourself an opportunity to write notes on the rehearsal process. You are allowed to take such notes (in the form of Context Summary Notes) into your unit 3 written exam, in which you will be asked to write on the process of rehearsing and performing this play. Therefore reflection and evaluation of the rehearsal process is vital to the success of that unit.

Notes

Don't launch straight into the text of the play. Try to use some early lessons and sessions to play games, to help the group bond and to create a good working atmosphere. Use some early sessions to workshop ideas and wider concepts based on themes, scenes, characters and performance styles. This is not wasted time: it will build a vocabulary of theatrical ideas to use on the text as you rehearse.

Make your rehearsals a positive and pleasant experience with a working atmosphere by:

Be positive

➢ Being on time

➢ Setting clear targets for the rehearsals

➢ Leaving the emotional baggage of your day at the studio/classroom door

➢ Putting aside personal grievances or relationship problems by focusing on the good of the play

➢ Bringing all the necessary equipment like your script, a pencil, a notebook and the right clothes to rehearse in

➢ Spending time thinking about the rehearsal before you arrive so that you are ready and willing to make creative contributions

➢ Spending a short time at the beginning of the rehearsal in a warm-up or playing a game to energise and focus.

➢ Seeing the rehearsal as work and treating the time as work time

➢ Being positive with each other and using positive language to praise work

➢ Always being constructive in criticism and avoiding personal comments. Try to talk about the work/character and how to improve this rather than the actual actor.

Above all, rehearsal should be great fun and should be enjoyed. Even the darkest and most serious of plays can still have a really enjoyable rehearsal process if everybody feels valued as a participant and is fully aware of what is trying to be achieved. It is important to make the whole process a shared responsibility.

Performing the play

Obviously the main rationale behind this performance is that it is an exam and part of your AS course, but you need to remember that it should also be a piece of theatre designed to entertain and engage an audience. The examiner will want to see a complete piece of theatre that has been well rehearsed, sensibly thought through and well presented.

Try to make the exam an occasion. Give it sense of completeness and significance. With this in mind, you need to really think about the following areas:

➢ **Where are you going to perform?** Will you be able to rehearse in your performance space? How will you use your performance space to meet the needs of the play best?

➢ **Who will be your audience?** You need an audience to make the play a valid piece of theatre. Will you target a certain age range for your production or will you look for a more general audience? Think carefully about your target audience as you rehearse the play.

➢ **Where will the examiner sit?** They will need a table and a table-lamp to write notes. You need to plan ahead as to where they should sit in order to get maximum access to the play with minimum disruption to the rest of the audience.

➢ **Make sure that the examiner can identify you within the performance.** It is sometimes conceptually appropriate for all the cast to wear black or dress similarly but this will not help the examiner. Think carefully about how you represent the characters within the play and allow time before the performance to meet with the examiner and let yourself be identified.

➢ **The play has to be videoed** so make sure you set a camera up well in advance and make sure that it has a good sight-line. It does not need to be a professional film of the show but just a simple record of the performance. This needs to be given to the examiner on the day or sent off shortly after.

Example play texts

Hopefully the advice above will be useful to you, but it is sometimes much easier to get ideas on how to work with a text if you have an actual example in front of you. Below you will find a detailed breakdown of how to work with two very different play texts for performance. You may choose (or may have already chosen) to use one of these texts for your own production, in which case you will find the information below very useful indeed! However, it can be just as helpful if you have decided on another text: the advice below on approaching the material is as generic as possible. This means that it should be easy to adapt to whatever text you are studying. When reading it through, consider how you could use the approaches below to help you when working on your chosen material.

The two plays discussed here, *Blue Remembered Hills* and *Grimm Tales*, have been chosen because of their contrasting styles, in order to give you an idea of the different approaches you can take in this unit. *Blue Remembered Hills* is essentially a realistic play – despite the fact it has adults playing the roles of young children – since it is vital that the audience believes in the characters if they are going to reflect on the themes of the production. *Grimm Tales* is a piece of very physical ensemble theatre which represents a set of

You should have provided a photograph of yourself in costume and you need to identify yourself on camera before the performance.

fantastical tales. You may wish to consider which is more similar to the piece you are working on.

Blue Remembered Hills

Blue Remembered Hills by Dennis Potter (1935–1994) was written for television and first broadcast in 1979. It is set in the West Country at the time of the second world war, during the long summer holiday of 1943.

Potter was one of television's most successful playwrights. He was passionate and controversial, inventive and reflective. He turned away from the traditions of theatre, realising that television was a more accessible and immediate form. He wanted to reach ordinary people in their own homes, while challenging the popular culture that dominated the scheduling.

His work explores concepts of religion, guilt, sexuality, infirmity and lost innocence, and reflects many of his own personal experiences. Having said this, it would be a mistake to describe his plays as autobiographical. They are reflections on issues that concern him and society as a whole. Although his style could be considered realistic at times, his manipulation of time, music and character often creates a dreamlike element to his work.

Blue Remembered Hills opens with the image of Willie, a seven-year-old boy, playing in a forest. His enjoyment is quickly interrupted by Peter, a thuggish child who threatens and intimidates him. Despite the conflict, they are clearly friends and the play follows their adventures on a summer's day. Seven children are introduced in all and there are frequent status battles as they fight for moments of supremacy. However, the play ends in tragedy, as their apparently harmless teasing leads to the character of Donald being burnt alive in a barn. The final image is of the children sitting in long grass, denying all knowledge of the events.

Blue Remembered Hills has many of the necessary elements for creating a successful AS-level performance:

➤ There is a good mixture of small group and ensemble scenes

➤ The mood of the play varies from humour to moments of pathos

➤ Each of the characters is defined clearly and with enough complexity to show a sense of development during the performance

➤ The concept of adults playing seven-year-olds ensures that decisions have to be made about vocal and physical work

➤ The notion of converting a television drama to a stage performance means that the use of design is very important.

Approaching the play

At the beginning of any rehearsal process, it is important to be clear about the challenges you are going to face. Start by asking yourself the following questions:

➤ How many lessons will we have to work on the script?

➤ Where could the piece be performed?

Further reading
Blue Remembered Hills by Dennis Potter (Samuel French 1990).

[Naturalism is] a stagnant pool where the spawn never turns into tadpoles, let alone frogs and princes.

Dennis Potter, Introduction to *Blue Remembered Hills*.

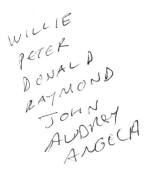

Why choose this play?

> ➤ Are any students doing design for the piece?
> ➤ How much direction is going to be offered by the teacher?
> ➤ Who is responsible for the casting of the play?

When making these decisions it is important to bear in mind the specific demands of the text. Therefore in your first group read-through it is vital to make notes on the characters and their given circumstances. This will ensure that all of your discussions remain tightly focused on the information that Potter conveys through his writing.

See the section on Stanislavski and his definition of given circumstances on pages 8–17.

In your group, read *Blue Remembered Hills*, including the author's note. Make notes on the individual characters, their age, appearance, behaviour and any factual references to their life. These given circumstances could also include their emotional reactions to any moments in the play. For example, your notes for the character of Raymond may look something like this:

> Raymond. Assumed to be seven years old. Wears cowboy hat and gun-belt. Stutters. Expressive face – often smiling. Owns a knife. Feels sympathy for animals. Is teased by Peter, Willie and occasionally John. Not always comfortable in the group of four boys. Relies on John for support. Wants to be a marine. Can stand on his head. When in the hollow, he wants to go home. Suggests they should scare Donald.

This factual information will provide you with the foundations for each rehearsal. Compile everyone's comments and make sure each person in the group has a copy.

Casting the play

It's important to cast the play carefully in order to ensure a balanced performance. Don't simply put your best performers in the biggest roles. Consider the demands of the characters and the physicality of the group. Peter needs to be a bully, burly and not too bright. Both Raymond and Donald are victims and need to be able to play low status and win the audience's sympathy. Angela is described as being 'pretty, with ringlet curls'; Audrey is 'plain' and manipulative. Willie needs to epitomise the playful spirit of children, constantly fidgeting and perhaps reminding the audience of themselves. John is the voice of reason – honest and fair – but he needs to stand a chance of beating Peter in a fight.

Take time over deciding who plays what. Ask other people for their opinions. You may want to play a character that is similar to yourself or you may want to act against type. It may be useful to ask members of your group to read scenes from the script so that you can hear how different voices work alongside each other.

Exploring the characters

Before beginning work on the text, it can be useful to experiment with the given circumstances. Now the play is cast, you can use the character information to improvise scenes, which will allow each individual to develop their role.

Status cards. Take a pack of cards and remove the jacks, queens, kings and jokers. The 40 cards that remain are going to be used to indicate the status of characters. Ten is extremely powerful, scared of no one. Ace is timid and unsure, unable to hold eye contact with others. Randomly distribute a card to each member of the group. Keeping their number secret, each person should now walk around the space as a seven-year-old with that status level, imagining they have just moved to a new school and know none of the other children. How would they react to the others? Avoid using any words and instead focus on the physical work. After two minutes of walking and meeting the other people, come out of character and try to order yourself based on what you have learnt from how other people have reacted to you. Create a line along one wall from highest to lowest status. Remember, up to four people could have the same numerical value; if someone feels they have the same value as another character then they should stand in front of them. Once everyone has decided on their position, reveal your cards.

Look at how successful you were as a group in conveying your status. Who should have had the most power in the room? Was this communicated?

In addition to showing levels of status, cards can be used to focus on the intensity of emotion. For example, ask two members of your group to improvise the following scenario as seven-year-olds. Before they begin, they will need to choose a card randomly. A is sitting on a school bench eating lunch. B approaches A and sits next to them. The numerical value of A's card indicates how intimidated they are by B's presence. B's card indicates how much they want to eat A's food. Repeat the scene with different actors and new numbers.

Imagine all seven characters are in the woods. They are about to play a game of grandmother's footsteps. The principle is simple. One person, A, stands facing a tree with their back to the rest of the group. The others stand in a line at the agreed starting point, which should be at least five metres away. Whenever A is facing the tree, the others can slowly creep towards them. However, A can turn round at any point and if they see anyone moving then that person is sent back to the start. The first person to touch A's back is the winner. Begin with the person who plays Peter explaining the rules to the others. Who might correct him if he gets confused? Who is likely to be facing the tree in the first game? Is anyone likely to cheat? Will anyone lose interest? Which character would be the worst loser? Use the game to explore character reactions.

Exercises like these are vital throughout the rehearsal process. The play relies on high energy both physically and mentally. As a group of actors, you need to be actively engaged in the rehearsal, and warm-up activities will help to ensure you remain focused during the lessons.

Staging the production

There are obvious difficulties in converting a television play into theatre. The script implies three different locations: a wood, a field and the interior of the barn, which might include a selection of

> " I used adult actors to play children in order to make them like a magnifying glass, to show what it's like. And because if you look at a child, talk about present tense, that's all they, all a small child, lives in. So a wet Tuesday afternoon can actually be years long. "
>
> Dennis Potter, Introduction to *Blue Remembered Hills*

Set design

tools and some hay. There is also a suggestion of levels (the hollow, the tree Peter falls from) and space (Audrey and Angela are seen in the distance, both the interior and exterior of the barn are needed from Scenes 25–28). When writing the play, Potter didn't want the audience to become lost in the realism of the piece; it was important to him that people reflected on the children's actions, finding parallels in their adult life. This needs to be considered in the staging of the piece and the positioning of the audience.

Before you begin rehearsing, it is important to discuss the needs of your piece. These are issues that the whole group should consider, even if one or more members are going to be responsible for the design aspects. Try focusing on the following points:

➤ How are you going to create a sense of the different locations? Are you going to do an open-air performance or try to bring elements of the outside into your space?

➤ How are the different areas created? Are there going to be distinct spaces or are you going to suggest the different locations through other means? For example, barn doors positioned centre-stage could imply the interior when opened but suggest the exterior when shut.

➤ Where are the audience going to be positioned? Remember you could choose from performing end-on (audience on one side), traverse (two sides), in the thrust (three sides), round (four sides) or promenade (audience walks to the action).

Colours, textures and even smells can help to recreate the feel of open fields, although you need to make sure that any flammable material is treated with fire retardant. If you are looking to design a non-realistic set, consider how you might try to capture the excitement of childhood.

Costume

Some of the play's reflective quality relies on the costume to create images and emotions from the past. The play is set in World War II and this backdrop of violence is essential to the action of the play. Therefore, when designing costume, it is important to be true to the period.

During this time, clothing was rationed and many outfits were hand-me-downs. Boys continued to wear shorts with knee socks, shirts with tank tops or jumpers. Girls wore plain knee-length dresses. Think how the clothing might reflect each character. Would any of the boys have their shirts tucked in? Is one costume dirtier than the others? What might colour say about a character? How might certain elements of costume add to key scenes?

Lighting

The demands of lighting the play will very much depend on the nature of the performance and the facilities available to you. Ideally, you should be looking to create two basic states – one for the woodland and one for the barn. In addition to this, the fire effect needs to be considered. If one member of your group has decided to specialise in lighting, there is a real opportunity to create a detailed design here.

The opening lighting state is one of bright sunshine. A general cover with straw-coloured gels would help to create this. If you are using a cyclorama as a backdrop, then this will need to be brightly

---

For more on these types of staging see pages 32–36.

Web link

See Kit Surrey's design at www.theatredesign.org.uk/arcdet/xkisu.htm. He uses ladders and a criss-cross of raised walkways to create the sense of locale.

In the original television production, Peter puts his jumper over the branch of a tree to simulate the parachute.

Web link

The stage electrics website has specific examples of gobos that are available: www.stage-electrics.co.uk

The international theatre design archive has images of lighting designs for various productions that could provide a reference point for your ideas: www.siue.edu/ITDA

lit. When Peter and Willie move deep into the woods in Scene 2, there is a chance to create a dappled effect using gobos. The intensity will probably need to be darker and there will be greater use of shadow and colour.

The barn could be darker still but with shafts of light, from a window gobo for example, to help create atmosphere. Work closely with the people responsible for set design in order to identify if specific areas need to be lit.

The creation of the fire in the barn needs to be striking. You could use a rotating gobo with different shades of red and orange to create the effect of a flickering fire. The intensity of the fire will need to increase and, depending on the positioning of the characters outside the barn, the light from the fire may need to be cast on them.

Sound

The level of sound you use in the piece will obviously depend on the specialist equipment available to you. However, several cues are essential in creating an appropriate mood and atmosphere. The claxon/siren and the sound of the fire are necessary for adding tension, and will need to be pre-recorded. The bird sounds could be used as a pre-recorded effect or replaced with a snapping twig or branch, adding to the woodland atmosphere. The poem at the end of the play could be spoken live, or be pre-recorded and even distorted to create a sense of the inappropriateness of such nostalgia.

The play also allows for the creation of a general soundscape for the woodland, which will provide continuous background noise throughout the scenes. This could be created by mixing together different tracks from the BBC Sound Effects CDs or by downloading effects from the Internet.

Web link

The BBC tracks will soon be available at the sound effects library in addition to their own resources at: www.sound-effects-library.com

Links between the scenes could be supported by certain classical tracks, which convey the sense of childhood spirit while defining changes in mood. The CD *Brian Kay's British Light Music Discoveries* (RBS conducted by Gavin Sutherland) is particularly successful in creating a sense of atmosphere and period.

Rehearsing

Organising rehearsals

There are 29 scenes in *Blue Remembered Hills*. Some of these are brief monologues by Donald; others are extremely complex passages of action with six or seven characters on stage at the same time. It is helpful to begin the process by dividing up your rehearsal time to ensure that all moments are given equal attention. Obviously there will be times when two scenes can be rehearsed simultaneously. For example, Scenes 4 and 6, in which Peter, Willie, John and Raymond shoot at the squirrel, can be rehearsed at the same time as Scene 5, in which Audrey, Angela and Donald are in the barn. If these scenes have been worked on during a week, then it would be useful to try to link the three together during the last session.

It is vital that you are clear about deadlines so that there is no confusion within your group. Make sure everyone knows when lines need to be learnt, when the first run-through will take place, and when designs will be presented. Allow time for a technical rehearsal and a dress rehearsal at the end of the process to ensure that the final performance to the examiner runs as smoothly as possible.

Rehearsing the text

Part of the success of your performance will undoubtedly lie in your ability to create truthful portrayals of seven-year-olds. The audience needs to believe in the action and emotion presented if they are going to reflect on their own behaviour. Therefore, one of the best ways of approaching the text is to use elements of Stanislavski's work (which is described in more detail on pages 8–17.) However, this is not the only method. We will look here at specific scenes from the play and will suggest different approaches. Many of the activities we suggest are generic and can be applied to any scene and, indeed, to any play. The key point to remember is that as actors you will need to embody your characters, and this is difficult to achieve if you simply spend each lesson reading the scene and then acting it out.

Rehearsal methods

Units and objectives

During rehearsal Stanislavski broke the play into temporary divisions called units; each new unit began where there was a change in the psychological state of the character. Once each unit had been worked on individually, they were linked back together demonstrating the emotional journey the characters followed during each scene.

Look at the following extract from Scene 1:

PETER   Give us a bit of thik apple, Willie.

WILLIE   *(trying to deflect his attention)* Your Uncle Arnold is a good parachuter.

PETER   Oy. Him is. Got medal and all. Hundreds and hundreds.

WILLIE   Do they keep their parachutes – bring 'um home, and that?

PETER   'Course they do!

He picks up a stone for no apparent reason, and hurls it away

         That's a good throw, that is. Near nigh half a bloody mile.

He sniffs

         Expect him'll bring I a parachute when him d'come home.

WILLIE   *(impressed)* Caw!

PETER   Two or dree if I d'want 'em. They be made of silk.

WILLIE   And sommat else is –

Willie sniggers. Peter looks at him suspiciously

PETER   Was mean?

WILLIE   Knickers is.

The two boys hoot and giggle. Then Peter's expression changes

PETER   I said give us a bit, didn't I?

WILLIE   *(reluctantly)* Him's a cooker, mind.

PETER   Wha-?

WILLIE   Cooking apple. And him yunt half sour. Honest.

PETER   Bist thou going to give I a bit or not

He stands straddle-legged over Willie, so far only half threatening

WILLIE   You can have the core.

PETER   And you can have my fist! What do I want with the flaming core, Willie?

WILLIE   Our dad says it's the best part of the apple.

PETER   Your dad is a loony, then.

In this short extract, there is a clear change in the relationship between Peter and Willie, but it is important to chart this change in terms of their mental state. Break this section into two separate units, using the point where Peter's expression changes as a natural divide. Give each character an objective for each unit remembering it must be in the form 'I want …'.

In the first unit Peter could want to impress Willie. This would affect not only the way he talks about the parachute but also the way he walks, sits and throws the stone. Willie could simply want to distract Peter. This could be emphasised by the way he listens overtly to Peter's claims while subtly hiding the apple behind his back. In the second unit, Peter wants to show his authority, and therefore his positioning and vocal tone need to be a lot more threatening. If Willie wanted to confuse Peter as a way of defending himself, he might speak at a faster pace but with an assured tone, moving around the performance area in an attempt to disorientate his friend.

 Work on both of these units playing the objectives to the full. Focus on the intention of each character for that moment of the text. If you don't feel it works, modify it to something that does.

The level of emotional detail in a scene can be made more complex by adding an adverb before each line. This addition is only temporary but helps to focus the actors' attention on the precise detail of each line. For example:

WILLIE   (**defiantly**) You can have the core.

PETER   (**aggressively**) And you can have my fist!

        (**suspiciously**) What do I want with the flaming core, Willie?

WILLIE   (**cautiously**) Our dad says it's the best part of the apple.

PETER   (**dismissively**) Your dad is a loony, then.

Write adverbs for each line of the text. Read through the units saying the adverb before speaking the line. This will help to reinforce the delivery. Once you have done this, act out the extract, trying to focus on the objective and the adverbs. Experiment with the extent to which the characters' thoughts are revealed on their faces.

Emotion memory

One of the advantages of acting a play in which the characters are younger than yourself is that you are able to recall your own experiences and feed them into your portrayal. Stanislavski wanted his actors to convey an emotional truth by using their emotion memory.

? Take a moment on your own to think about your memories of childhood. Think of warm summer days. Think of moments you spent by yourself. Try to recall where you went, what you did, how it made you feel. Think of the sights, the sounds and the smells. Who used to intimidate you when you were younger? Was there anyone of a similar age to you? What did they do to make you feel uncomfortable? How did you react? Did you knowingly intimidate others? Can you remember why?

You may wish to talk within your group about these experiences or keep the thoughts to yourself. Use these memories in your performance to intensify Peter and Willie's relationship. You may also find the visual images you created useful in communicating a sense of locale to the audience.

Status games   We've already looked at how status games can be used in the early stage of rehearsal to develop character. Now that you have a clearer sense of the play, it is appropriate to apply similar ideas to the text. Scene 5 ('The old barn') in many ways epitomises the structure of the entire play. Initially the audience will probably take pleasure from the idyllic image of childhood. The barn in itself has a sense of magic to it and the image of two girls playing mummies and daddies with the comic Donald has real appeal. During the scene, however, Potter cleverly manipulates this response, so that Audrey and Angela turn and start picking on Donald rather than each other.

The scene focuses on the change in allegiance and how having good ideas during play can help you to belong to a group. Therefore, a good way into the scene is to look at who is isolated at any one point.

The actors playing Donald, Angela and Audrey should position three chairs at an equal distance apart from each other in the shape of a triangle. Each character should begin the scene standing by a different chair. However, once you start acting the script, if any character feels drawn to another they should move to that person's chair. Only two people can stand by any given chair at one time, although a character could move from their chair to an empty chair, if one exists, in order to increase their status. Try rehearsing the scene with the rest of your group, monitoring who moves and when.

Hopefully, it should become clear that Donald moves back and forth between the two girls as they vie for his attention, before Angela's jealousy causes her to turn on him. This should provide a foundation for the action in your scene. Work on having Audrey and Angela on opposite ends of the stage while Donald moves between them or stands on his own. Develop this even further by improvising a game of piggy-in-the-middle, in which Audrey and Angela throw the ball to each other while Donald attempts to steal it from them. Initially, they shouldn't mind if Donald gets the ball, but see how competitive they can become as the game develops.

The lines in this scene generally split into two different styles: those that are said as part of their game and those that are spoken out of their role as seven-year-olds trying to determine the rules of their creative play. The latter can be spoken quite aggressively, in a deliberate attempt to reduce the other person's status in the scene. This helps to reinforce the fragile, fluctuating nature of the children's power and creates a real sense of character development in quite a short scene.

Each actor in the scene should draw a graph for their character with status marked 1 to 10 on one axis and time on the other axis. Decide on an initial status level using the guidance given earlier in this chapter. Then look at key lines spoken by the characters that will either raise or lower status. Plot these points in chronological order on your graph, indicating any changes in your status level. Note the final status at the end of the play.

This is quite a formal way of structuring your scene and in some ways can appear a little forced. However, it does allow you to identify specific moments of dramatic interest and to focus on how vocal delivery and movement might alter during these status changes.

Physicalising the text

The television version of *Blue Remembered Hills* has the luxury of being able to use wide-open fields and different camera angles in order to convey the sense of childhood adventure. Your performance is obviously going to be restricted by space. There may be a tendency to become lazy and simply position yourself randomly on stage, but in order to achieve good marks for your performance you need to show a very strong command of movement through gesture, poise and stillness.

Scene 6, with the dead squirrel, is an example of three pages of dialogue in which the focus remains the same. The skill is to ensure that there is plenty of movement, from subtle childish fidgets to bold gestures, and frequent changes in the physical dynamic between the characters.

If you know any seven-year-olds, try to find an opportunity to observe their behaviour. Note how their physicality changes when they are playing by themselves and when they are communicating in a group. Use this to help you give a more truthful performance.

In your group make a list of different children's gestures and movements. This could include how they sit, stand and walk, as well as how they communicate with their body while talking or any small mannerisms that they adopt unconsciously. Which movements would be most appropriate for which character? Build up a language of gestures on which you can draw at different points in the play.

Childish patterns of behaviour need to be supplemented with more structured images in order to show a command of mood and atmosphere. This is where it is vital that you work as a whole group, watching each other's performances in an attempt to tighten the physical impact of your work on the audience.

Image sculpting. Imagine that the actors playing Peter, Willie, John and Raymond are blobs of clay. The other members of the group are sculptors who need to create a series of emotions. Obviously each emotion will be presented as a still image so the 'blobs' need to be positioned carefully in order to ensure maximum effect on the audience. Think about using different levels, moving round the acting space and exaggerating facial expressions. Assume that the squirrel is always positioned centre-stage. Sculpt each of the following, bearing in mind the four characters and the need for significant changes in movement: excitement, guilt, disgust, reverence, laughter.

Once you have worked on each of the five images, the four actors should try moving from one to the other, paying real attention to detail and making the transition as smooth as possible. Next, look at the script and note that the emotions are a way of charting the changes in mood during the scene. Try to identify the most appropriate moment for each image. Once you have done this, rehearse the entire scene, making sure you form the images at the agreed point. Think about making the movement a natural progression during the dialogue.

Vocalising the text

In order to score highly in your performance, you will need to demonstrate a very strong command of voice through clarity, pause, pace, inflection and projection. It is important that you show a range in your delivery that appears natural to the character. A forced example of each skill for every character in every scene is inappropriate and will not be rewarded by the examiner.

Look at Scene 14, 'The Hollow'. The stage directions run as follows: 'The five plunge for safety into a natural, grassy, scooped-out hollow in the midst of the trees. They huddle together, breathless and scared.' The lack of movement in the opening of this scene should focus your attention on vocal skills. John, Raymond, Willie, Angela and Audrey are confined to a small space. John's status has raised to the position of leader because he won the fight, although he appears slightly uncomfortable in the role. Vocally, you will need to begin by creating a sense of childhood fear, which will always be present to some degree. In addition to this, you should experiment with moments which might subtly alter the tone of delivery. Try each of the following activities in turn as a way of experimenting with the text.

 Sitting on chairs and with pencils in hand, read the script from the start of the scene to just before Peter's entrance. You are not allowed to pause between lines. Any changes in pace need to be created by the delivery of the lines themselves. Once you have read it through, go back to the start and repeat the exercise two more times. In between each reading, do not talk about which moments were most successful; try different ideas while you are reading and hearing the script. Once the exercise has been completed three times, discuss among the group where you think the pace naturally increases or slows. Mark these areas on your text.

 Now try exploring the use of pause in the scene. Position yourself on the floor as if you are in the hollow. Keeping the same decisions about pace, repeat the scene three times, focusing on natural breaks that can be made in the dialogue. Some are indicated by Potter's use of stage directions, but don't slavishly rely on these: find an interpretation that works for you. Once the group has found moments for pause, discuss how long these could be. Some might be no more than a natural beat between lines to add

---

Rehearsal tip

The West Country accent is not essential but it is useful in creating the sense of the magical past. Try experimenting with it in the early stages of rehearsal. Be brave. You may find it improves naturally.

Design factors

There are practical difficulties in staging the hollow. The small, cramped space can create difficulties with audience sight-lines. Look at using small changes in levels (crouching, sitting, lying) as a way of allowing all of the children's expressions to be seen.

---

emphasis; others might be a long moment of silence, adding to the fear, excitement or humour of the situation. During the pauses in dialogue, experiment with smirks, sighs, anxious breaths and other sounds that could add to the mood of the scene.

Varying your vocal tone in this scene is vital. All of the characters show different shades of emotion and these need to be represented by your inflection. Look at the following extract:

AUDREY You're not frightened. Are you?

JOHN 'Course not!

AUDREY Wallace Wilson 'ood go up and have a look.

JOHN In a minute, I said. Shut your mouth, Audrey.

AUDREY Oy – and Peter would an' all.

JOHN *(muttering)* Shut your cakehole.

In pairs, rehearse this section for a few minutes, making sure each line is performed with a slightly different tone. Perform each of the versions to the rest of the group, noting the differences in vocal delivery. Clearly Audrey is trying to undermine John's power, partly because she can sense his fear. John is trying to defend his position but, depending on how you interpret his 'muttering', he could be totally unsuccessful.

Understanding these variations in tone is vital in ensuring that the scene remains fresh and interesting for the audience. A way of quantifying these changes could be to look at the characters' levels of fear during the scene by using the numbers 1 to 10 (1 being 'petrified'). Identify when they might grow in confidence. What words might make them more paranoid?

Communication

Out of the 80 marks for this unit, 30 are available for your ability to communicate with your fellow actors and with the audience. The latter is particularly important and, in consultation with your group, your teacher will need to submit a directorial aim that identifies the elements of the play on which you have chosen to focus. Since the examiner will use this as a guide when marking your piece, it is important that you spend some time considering this area.

It was essential to Potter that his play didn't create an image of an idyllic childhood. Children can be sweet and innocent but they can also be vindictive and cruel. The world of seven-year-olds has the potential to be endearing but also repulsive. His insistence on adult actors served as a magnifying glass and also a barrier, distancing the audience from retrospective sentiment when confronted with the image of children playing. The play is not about the past, but is an image of us in the present and our reactions to the world around us. Potter emphasises this in his introduction:

> The fear of being mugged that I suddenly felt when stupidly walking at night in one of the many wrong parts of New York was almost exactly the same fear I had felt four decades earlier about being waylaid by one particular bully in the high-hedged lanes which led away from my Forest of Dean primary school. And I

In the BBC production, Willie, played by Colin Welland, takes great joy from wriggling during one of the pauses as he tries to adjust his position. This creates humour through his childish sniggering and the frustration of the others.

> "The stories we read in childhood have a potency that cannot be destroyed, not even by the nostalgia which is normally the most powerful disinfectant known to man. "
>
> Dennis Potter, Introduction to *Blue Remembered Hills*

did not want these, or any other, emotions to be distanced by the presence of young limbs, fresh eyes and falsetto voices.

This sentiment is most evident at the end of the play when both the horror of Donald's fate and the naturally dishonest response of the children work side by side. Potter finishes the play with the A. E. Housman poem, from which the play's title is taken, which is a longing for those lost years of childhood. The poem glorifies the past and idealises childhood, and is strikingly ironic when played over the top of the children sobbing in the field.

Throughout your performance it is important to balance the apparently conflicting elements of the excitement and the tragedy of childhood. The audience should find some of the violence comical – in many ways this is a natural reaction. However, as the play progresses and the actions become more vindictive, the audience is encouraged to question not only their reactions but also their adult behaviour.

Grimm Tales

The German brothers Jacob and Wilhelm Grimm collected and recorded their stories in the early 1800s, and the first handwritten collection dates from 1810. Many of their stories have become ingrained within our own culture, through Disney and other films, theatre, pantomime, television and stories read to us as children. It is likely that you have knowledge of many of their collected tales without realising their origin. The Brothers Grimm are responsible for collecting and telling versions of such famous stories as *Sleeping Beauty*, *Snow White*, *Hansel and Gretel*, *Cinderella* and *Red Riding Hood*.

The dramatisation of the tales was originally produced and performed at the Young Vic Theatre in London in 1994. The Young Vic has always been a theatre committed to exciting young people about theatre.

 Watch some film versions of the stories of the Brothers Grimm to see how they can be both sanitised and made accessible for children, as well as darkened to explore the more serious and sinister sides of the stories. Contrast Disney's *Snow White and the Seven Dwarves* with *Snow White: a Tale of Terror* (directed by Michael Cohn and starring Sigourney Weaver).

Another recommendation would be to watch Neil Jordan's film *The Company of Wolves*, based on Angela Carter's re-telling of Red Riding Hood, which has a very stylised and theatrical approach and may help you with ideas in the later process of interpretation and staging.

Plot summary The play text deals with eight of the stories of the Brothers Grimm, originally adapted by Carol Ann Duffy and then dramatised by Tim Supple and the Young Vic Company. The stories all play independently with a clean beginning and ending, and the text offers no framing device to link the stories together. It was felt that

Further reading
Grimm Tales – adapted from the Brothers Grimm by Carol Ann Duffy, dramatised by Tim Supple (Faber and Faber 1996).

Web link
It's worth visiting the Young Vic website at www.youngvic.org to get an idea about their approach to theatre, their history and specific information about *Grimm Tales*.

Further reading
Try the section in the back of Rob Brannen's *Tales Untold* (Hodder Arnold, 1999), which answers some key questions about the Brothers Grimm. See also *More Grimm Tales* (Faber and Faber 1997), which includes clear background notes by Craig Higginson.

a link was provided by using the same group of actors to tell all the stories. The stories in order are:

Hansel and Gretel	A dark and nightmarish story concerning two young children who are abandoned in a forest because their parents no longer have enough food to keep them. There they meet and defeat an evil witch before returning to their home to face their parents.
The Golden Goose	A funny and farcical tale of three sons. One son, with the help of a little grey magic man, discovers a goose with golden feathers. His goose attracts the attentions and desires of a range of people, who through their greed become stuck to the goose in a long chain. The ending is a happy one that involves a king, a princess who can't laugh and a wedding.
Ashputtel	A dark and poetic tale that is similar in story to the better-known Cinderella, in that it concerns an oppressed girl, love, a horrible stepmother and sisters, a ball and a rescuing prince.
A Riddling Tale	A short narrative puzzle that was used in the original production to end the first half by leaving the audience with a question, and to start the second half by answering it. The examiners advise against the use of intervals, so it may be difficult to use this tale.
The Mouse, the Bird and the Sausage	A dark, comic tale about friendship and greed between a mouse, bird and sausage. In the original production a single narrator told it as a puppet show. This could be possibly explored using people as the marionettes.
Iron Hans	A dark, poetic, rites of passage story about a young prince who disobeys his parents and is forced to live in anonymity with a magical figure in the forest, who is able to grant him help and wishes. He is forced to solve a series of problems and go to war before eventually finding love and peace again.
The Lady and the Lion	A tale about love that is similar in ingredients to the better-known Beauty and the Beast. It sets the theatrical problem of presenting animals and abstract concepts such as the Sun, the Moon and the Wind.
The Magic Table, the Gold-Donkey and the Cudgel in the Sack	A magical and funny story that lifts the end of the play with a celebration of theatricality. Complete with a shitting-and-spitting donkey, the play traces a small and poor community's deserving rise from rags to riches.

Why choose this play?

This type of play offers up wonderful flexibility for casting. It was originally performed by seven actors – four men and three women. However, because the cast took on more than one role and played a variety of parts in each story, there is plenty of room to create a bigger company by sharing parts or changing and sharing the narrative lines. The play also allows for cross-gender casting because of the style of performance and the way in which characters can be represented and portrayed.

It is a text that will also allow an ensemble of actors to work together and show some of the mechanisms of theatre, in that they can represent not only characters but also inanimate objects, animals and even become the set itself.

The play also offers clear opportunities for sensible cutting to meet the time constraints. Because there are eight stories you can select the stories you would like to perform in order to meet the time constraints of the exam, and yet still give a varied and coherent performance. It also gives you significant opportunities for theatricality in response to the exam criteria for assessment.

Casting

In this text actors need to tell a story as clearly as possible, working with their voices, their bodies, the space around them and their relationship with each other. It does not need a set and props but demands that the actors challenge the audience's imagination and engage them in a fictional world. This type of text is liberating for the actor but also incredibly challenging, as there is very little to hide behind. It will allow you to explore and apply Brechtian ideas of storytelling.

Time constraints

> [Duffy's] work was to draw from each story its particular linguistic qualities and to give the language the simple rhythms of speech. Our task was then to give each story a particular theatrical shape. Decisions on who would speak and who would do what were based partly on our perceptions of the style or form demanded by each story and partly on the particular talents of the performers in our company.
>
> Supple, introduction to *Grimm Tales.*

See pages 32–36 for more on these types of staging.

Practical work

There are many other similar plays that you could work on, according to the approach laid out below. When you feel you have understood the style of approach needed for storytelling ensemble theatre you can be confident that you can apply this approach to a whole range of texts.

Approaching the play

The text *Grimm Tales* is split into two very distinct sections. The second section is a collection of the eight stories adapted by Duffy. These are the story texts that provided the material for Tim Supple and the Young Vic Company to rehearse with. The first section contains the final dramatisations of the eight stories.

You have to remember that the text you are reading was specially created for a known group of actors who worked on the stories before they created the play text. You need to use this approach to some degree when you start rehearsing the play. Consider the same specific questions that the original company would have faced:

How long do we have to rehearse?

Make sure that you break your rehearsal time down into sections. You need to plan your time so that you have: some general introductory sessions to explore the style of the play; some specific time allocated to each of the stories that you have chosen; time to bring all the stories together in a final coherent play; time for technical rehearsal in the performance space.

How many of us are in the group and will anyone be taking on a design role?

The play text is written for four men and three women, and though it would be easy to make the cast bigger and change the gender of roles it would take some time and thought to do this.

What space will you be performing in?

Make sure you are aware of the dimensions of the space that you are working in and where the audience will be sitting. This will significantly affect the way you present the piece. Will the audience be at one end of the space? Will they wrap around you in the round? Will your playing space have the audience on three sides, as in a thrust configuration? What about using a promenade to walk your audience to different locations for different stories? What about using a traverse style and having the audience on two sides with a passageway along which the stories can appear and then disappear?

Exploring the style of the play

The best way to begin exploring a script like *Grimm Tales* is through practical work. You will set the tone for all rehearsals, since practical work will be vital to the shaping of an ensemble and physical play. Successful rehearsals can only be achieved if the cast are really focused and support each other in practical work. And you may well solve casting problems by allowing people to shine in certain improvisations or realise that certain parts are not for them.

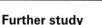

The key to creativity is activity. The only way you will invent practical ideas and find solutions to any staging and movement problems that are thrown up by the text is to have a vocabulary of movement ideas that you have already explored or a willingness to try new ideas. Both these approaches can be engendered in early workshop sessions.

 You should spend some time, even if it is just a couple of lessons, looking at the stories in their adapted format as written by Carol Ann Duffy.

Read 'The Golden Goose' story with your group.

> Now choose between six and 12 still images that you think best represent the chronology of the story, using just your bodies and the space you are working in. Make sure the images have a clear focus in terms of what part of the story they are representing. Make each image very different. Try to involve everyone in the image even if they are not a character: turn people into objects, trees, buildings and even the goose.

> Now give each image a caption or title before you move into it. Get a different person in your group to contribute a title so that you get used to sharing the narration, having different points of narration, and also being both a narrator and a character.

> Now begin to use physical movement to link each of the images. These movements can reflect what happens in the story between the selected images or can just be a piece of choreographed fun reflecting the mood of the piece.

> Now introduce thought-tracking for one of the characters. This is when one of the characters will speak out loud about what he or she is thinking at that moment in time. This should reveal a little about the character and will also test the actor's understanding of what is going on beneath the action.

> Now introduce some dialogue into one of the pictures. Choose some of the dialogue that you think is vital and important to the sense or significance of the story.

> Now try to introduce a movement sequence that deals with an event in the story. You can choose an event that happens at any point but it must be an event that will be communicated more clearly through images than words.

> Now try to run through a performance of the story using all the elements that you have explored above, working hard at making the story make sense.

This style of approach early in the rehearsal process will allow you the freedom and confidence to apply physical actions and create images to support the text.

Early props and staging

Choosing key elements of staging and props early in the rehearsal process can be incredibly liberating for an ensemble physical-theatre piece of storytelling. If you work from the beginning with a key element of staging then it can quickly become an integral part of the physical representation of the story.

It is important not to clutter the space with realistic representations of the setting or furniture of the worlds that you are trying to create. It is better to rely mainly on the actors, their voices, their bodies and the space to create the imaginary world of the tale. However, it can be really beneficial to use a key piece of staging or prop to support the work of the actors.

 Wee Stories is a theatre company based in Scotland that works primarily for children. They have developed a very unique way of working on texts, centring on the importance of key props. They recently devised and performed a piece based on the legend of King Arthur in which they used cornflake boxes as a central staging device for the whole story: the boxes became characters, the knight's helmets, Stonehenge and even Camelot.

They have a simple philosophy towards props which can be really useful when working in a style where minimal use of props is essential to the imaginary world being created. Props can only be used if they have the following values:

Royal Prop. This is a prop that must be used more than once as different things. In 'Hansel and Gretel' it could be a stick that acts as the mother's broomstick but go on to be the woodcutter's axe, the witch's walking stick and a large stirring spoon for the witch's pot.

Golden Prop. This a special prop that is essential to the story and used only once. In 'The Golden Goose' this could be the goose itself.

If you consider and evaluate the props you use in this way you will begin to rationalise their use and support the minimalist approach that such a style of storytelling demands.

 Try working on the story of 'Hansel and Gretel' in its adapted format as written by Duffy.

Try to find a large rectangular table or, even better, a large trunk or storage box with a lid that will take the weight of an actor. After reading the story, try to improvise it but use the table or box to represent key locations and props within the story. Try to use it differently for each thing, by placing it at a different angle or in a different stage space, or by turning it over or on its end. Do this every time it occurs in the story so that an audience would begin to recognise what the object was supposed to be when in a specific location or shape.

Set yourself the problem of using the box/table in a different way as each of the following:

➤ The door to Hansel and Gretel's house

➤ The bed in which their mother and father sleep

➤ The house itself

➤ A tree branch

➤ The wood fire

➤ The window of the witch's house

➤ The shed in which Hansel is imprisoned

➤ The oven.

Web link

More information on the way they work and about past productions is available at www.weestoriestheatre.org.

Framing   The concept of framing is concerned with who is telling the story. If you are dealing with a play text that is a series of stories it may help to consider who is telling those stories, to find a link between them in order to make one coherent play. For example, in Michael

Bogdanov's adaptation of *The Canterbury Tales* he uses the original author Chaucer's idea of the pilgrims having a competition to tell the best story. This enables characters and relationships to develop outside of the stories as well as within them.

With *Grimm Tales* there is no framing device. However, if you are selecting only a number of the stories you may wish to consider adding a framing device to help their continuity and coherence.

> We found we did not need any formal means of tying the stories together, no frame or thread or justification was necessary: the collection itself, the event of one group telling all the stories, was enough.
>
> Supple, in the notes to *Grimm Tales*.

 It may help you to think about the following things:

➤ Who is telling these stories, and to whom

➤ The period when the stories were originally composed and by whom

➤ The oral tradition of the stories, how they were passed down and on what occasions they would be told

➤ How stories are told today by parents to their children

➤ The message of the stories and why they are being told.

Creating a frame for a play text that is composed of many stories can be a gateway into finding a style for the performance and designing the staging that will be used.

One such frame for *Grimm Tales* could be a mother or granny telling children stories before bedtime. The children clamour for a story and a story is told. They then want another story and another story is told. Perhaps the children request a style of story: 'We want a funny story, Grandma!', 'We want a love story, Grandma!', 'We want a scary story, Grandma!'. The context is a bedroom, and the set for the bedroom is a bed and a chair. These then become the 'royal' props of the stories that must use these props in different ways. The materials and sheets on the bed could also become a part of the storytelling.

This frame forces the audience to use their imagination, but also allows the props to become a large number of other things for a clear reason: namely they are being used because the people telling the story – Grandma and the children – are using the objects available to them in their real world to create the world of the imaginary story.

Rehearse the following framed scene. A child is being read a story by their parent. The improvisation begins with the parent saying 'and they all lived happily ever after. Now goodnight, and don't you worry about witches and monsters.' The child falls asleep but as they sleep their dream comes to life and you improvise a fairy story, which includes the witches and monsters that have just been read to them – but with the child in the story. Your only staging is the bed that you created from a block, table or bench and the materials that you have used for bedcovers.

Perhaps you could finish the improvisation by hinting that even now the child has woken up, part of the dream world has come with them: the parent could say a notable line from the dream or do something that one of the characters in the dream did.

Framing stories can be great fun but you should set aside just one session early on to explore the notion of who is telling the stories and how. You may decide not to create a frame: see what works for you and your group.

Designing the production

The problem in staging a play such as *Grimm Tales* is that you are trying to create a neutral space in which to tell different stories as well as a fantastical space in which each story can have an atmosphere and reality of its own. This dual purpose can be resolved by keeping the space uncluttered and working with a simple and minimalist staging style. This allows the words and the characters to conjure the mood and the atmosphere of the stories.

Obviously the way in which the stories are written and the words that are used are incredibly helpful in staging the stories. They tell us **who** the characters are, **where** they are, and indicate the **mood** of the moment through the way in which the characters speak.

 Look at the opening of the Ashputtel story and try the following tasks:

➤ Read the first three speeches out loud.

➤ Now read the speeches again but get three actors from your group to mime the roles of the father, mother and young girl.

➤ Repeat this but use another member of your group to create an atmospheric soundscape to the scene, such as angelic humming, crying, wind and so on.

➤ Repeat the scene again and use another member of your group to become the other elements of the story such as the bed, the grave and the snow.

Solving these staging problems using only the resources of the actor – their voice, body and the space – will not only help meet the demands of the differing stories, but will also help you maximise your scoring potential when the examiner is assessing you.

There are other ways of solving the staging problems of a text such as *Grimm Tales* that can work in partnership with the physical theatre ideas and even embellish and support that style. These methods can be particularly useful if you have people in your group wanting to take on design skill roles.

Set design

Fantastic stories can provide the potential for fantastic sets. The recent production of *Shockheaded Peter* – based on the German story of Struwwelpeter written and illustrated by Heinrich Hoffman in the 1880s – shows the potential for creating such a fantastic set. The play is set in a huge Victorian doll's house echoing themes of childhood, play and stories, but also hinting at something a little darker. The piece uses the rooms, windows, doors and even floorboards to reveal and present the story.

You could attempt to create a set of imagination and sophistication yourself but you may not have the space, resources and time to do so. Your starting-point must be a consideration of these elements, as well as an awareness of the demands of the play text and group

Web link

See www.shockheadedpeter.com for more on this production.

of actors you are working with. If the actors are working in a simple physical theatre storytelling style then what should you provide for them? The answers to these questions always lie in the text. Look at the text and find out:

➢ Where is the story located?

➢ When is the story set?

➢ Are there any specific elements of the set that are required? A table, or a door, for example?

 List the stories and explore the location/period/specific demands. For example:

Hansel and Gretel: • A sense of the past • A sense of another country • A bed, a house, a forest, a witch's house, a shed, an oven.

Once you have analysed the functional requirements of the text, you can begin to make artistic decisions about how to interpret these demands. Remember that the space should be both neutral (for between stories) and individually fantastical (for each story): keep the playing areas as clear as possible and choose key elements of set and props that are integral to each story and can be both real and representative. A design that would demonstrate considerable imagination and sophistication would involve one key piece of staging that can become central to all the stories and be used differently in each.

 The exam board also has specific demands in regards to this skill. As a set designer, you must create:

➢ A portfolio of research and sketches showing the development of your ideas

➢ A 1:25 scale model of the final design

➢ A 1:25 scale ground plan and scale drawing of any designed props

➢ A justification for the final design decisions

➢ The design as realised in the performance.

You must also take a lead role in the supervision, construction, painting, hiring and/or finding of any of the scenic elements.

The problem with designing costumes for a play text such as *Grimm Tales* is that no definite ideas or directions are supplied. However, there are plenty of clues within the stories, their background and the style of the performance that will allow you to make decisions about what to wear.

Consider the clues under these three headings:

The staging of the stories. You will have noted already that if you are going to take an ensemble approach your group of actors will need to play more than one part in each story and a variety of parts in all the stories. This will generally mean that you cannot be

The original Young Vic production was played in the round with no specific setting and very few props. The wooden-plank texture of the floor created the background and natural feel required for the production and the focus at all times was on the action, the words and the characters that spoke them.

Costume design

anchored in one costume because the audience will become confused as to who you are. If you are working on a framing device then you will need a basic costume for your neutral character in that framing device. You will need to continue that basic costume between stories so that you are not confused with a character from one of them. The characters in each story will need to be represented clearly to the audience so that they can clearly follow the action and relationships, despite knowing and understanding that they are being played by a small company of actors.

Bearing all this in mind, costume selection should allow a basic outfit that can have additional costumes added to it to indicate characters. The costumes become **emblems** to describe each character and need to be chosen carefully to represent them.

The background of the stories. The stories are European in origin, and were collected and recorded in the early 1800s. This could be reflected in the basic costume and in the additional costume. This sense of period and location roots the work in its source, and shows an understanding of when it was written and who was writing it.

However, the themes and issues that the stories deal with are just as relevant today as when they were originally told and collected, so you could easily put some or all of the tales in a modern context with modern costumes. Doing so makes a firm statement that the stories are about now and not just the past, and is an equally valid way of working.

The specifics of the action within the story. There are specific costume demands within the stories, since characters such as kings, princesses and warriors will need clear representation. There are also some specific directions within the texts, for example regarding the use of cloaks in Ashputtel.

There are some characters (such as the Lion Prince and the Dragon Princess in 'The Lady and The Lion', the goose in 'The Golden Goose' and the goat and the donkey in the final tale) that will need clear but imaginative representation through costume or prop. There is also a sense of mood that needs to be conveyed through costume, from the dark and nightmarish quality of 'Hansel and Gretel' through to the farce-like 'The Golden Goose'.

Collect together any old jackets, waistcoats, coats, skirts and so on that you are able to locate at home, school or from charity shops. Place them around a space within the classroom or the studio. Gather your group in the centre of the space and begin to read out loud 'The Golden Goose'.

Each time you play a character within the story you must find an item of clothing that best represents them, and when you are not playing a character you must remove that item and support the scene by becoming bits of scenery or props.

The goose must also be made from the clothing: for example, a jacket turned inside-out with the arm representing the neck of the goose. Your task here is to be clear in representing characters, but also to enjoy the humour of quick changes and show the mechanisms of theatrical representation.

You need to show a real clarity in representing characters and types of characters. As with the staging, keeping it simple and clear will enhance the overall performance and your potential to score marks.

 The exam board also has specific demands regarding this skill. As a costume designer, you must create:

➢ A portfolio of research and sketches showing the development of ideas

➢ A final design for all the characters in the production (must be a minimum of three)

➢ A justification for the final design decisions

➢ A costume plot with a list of costumes/accessories worn by the actors and an indication of when they change

➢ A demonstration of the costumes within the performance.

➢ You must also supervise the construction, buying, dyeing, altering, hiring and/or finding of any of the designed costumes, but you only need to carry out one of the tasks yourself.

The beauty of a text such as *Grimm Tales* is that the power of the tales is in the telling – the events, the words and the characters conjure all that is necessary. A piece such as this could be performed outside in daylight or in a room or studio under normal lighting. However, if you have access to theatre lighting then there is plenty of potential to use it.

As with set and costumes, the lighting should support the style of storytelling and not upstage the stories. Keep the lighting simple and clear. Your primary concern when designing the lighting for such a piece is to make one good general state which lights evenly and well. The majority of the storytelling will be told in this light. This light will represent the neutrality of the story and allow the actors to work at using the words and themselves to create mood.

There is, however, plenty of opportunity to enhance the stories within the play.

The key questions to consider when thinking about lighting the play and scenes within it are:

➢ Where is the scene located? A forest as in 'Hansel and Gretel' or 'The Lady and the Lion'?

➢ What time of day is it? Day or night as in 'Hansel and Gretel'?

➢ Is there a particular mood being created? Scary or sad as in 'Iron Hans', for example?

➢ Are there any effects within the scene that need to be supported by lighting? The mother dying in 'Ashputtel', for example, or the transition from monster to human in 'The Lady and the Lion'?

In the fantastical world of the story, lighting can be a major contributor to all the above questions. By varying the intensity of light, the gel colour and the angle used, a whole array of states can be created to convey meaning.

Lighting design

Set up a single floor flood lantern at the front of a space, a single but general white lantern above the space, a general lantern that has a blue gel and one that has a red gel.

The floor flood will cast excellent shadows and create good atmospheric lighting if kept at a low volume; the blue will indicate night; and the red will indicate an evil or wicked presence or mood. The white will be the normal storytelling light.

Now improvise the story of Hansel and Gretel. Don't worry about being too accurate with words at this stage: just allow the lighting to explore and support the various states that the improvisation passes through. This should help you to make decisions about what lighting works and what doesn't.

 The exam board also has specific demands regarding lighting. As a lighting designer, you must create:

➢ A portfolio of research and sketches showing the development of ideas

➢ The final lighting design with a grid plan and lantern schedule that indicates the use of at least two different kinds of lantern and uses a minimum of 16 lanterns

➢ A justification for the final lighting design

➢ A lighting plot or cue sheet showing at least six different lighting states

➢ A demonstration of the lighting plot within the context of the performance.

You must supervise the rigging, focusing and operating of the design, but you need only carry out one of the tasks yourself.

Rehearsing

Organising rehearsals

Due to the time constraints laid out by the exam board, you will need to choose three or four of the original eight *Grimm Tales*. The dramatised tales you choose will not necessarily be of equal length or demand equal amounts of rehearsal time so you need to be careful when apportioning time. Try to view the work in three phases:

Phase 1 – Early exploration

You need to set aside time just to work on the style of staging. This should be done early, and should involve exploring the adapted stories that exist in the second half of the play text as suggested earlier. You should also set aside some time to think about and explore framing the stories within a context. It is during this period that you should introduce elements of staging, props and costumes and also experiment with voices, bodies and the space. You also need to make final decisions about casting.

Phase 2 – Tackling the tales

This is the heart of the rehearsal process, the phase in which you explore the narration and the characters and their dialogue, help each other understand the intent of the scene and begin to detail blocking to enable an audience to engage with the work and enjoy and understand the story.

Phase 3 – Polish and performance

This is the final phase, when you really begin to glue the stories together and see the relationship between them and the characters that you play in all of them. It is a time to make sure you have constructed one whole play rather than many smaller ones, and a time to secure the design elements of the performance.

 Always set a clear target and objective for each rehearsal and agree what that is at the beginning of each session. If the teacher is taking some or all responsibility for the direction then it is still relevant to discuss what you want to have achieved by the end of the session. This helps to keep people focused on the task and gives a sense of moving towards achieving something.

 Try to integrate design ideas early so that you are working with staging, props, costume and to some degree lighting and sound, in order to avoid these becoming add-ons rather than an important part of how the performance evolves.

 Make a log of all rehearsals and use the agreed target as the heading for each entry. You can evaluate the success of what you achieved against what you wanted to achieve. You can begin to analyse why things did or didn't go well.

Rehearsal methods

The text

Grimm Tales demands certain performance skills. The text requires you to give clear, neutral narration, but also to assume and create wonderful characterisation. Often this transformation will take place in front of the audience. The text will demand the creation of staging objects and animals with just your voices, bodies and the space.

Duality

Look at the father's speech in 'Hansel and Gretel', from 'It was no more than once upon a time…' through to '…a voice as fierce as famine'. Read through the speech a couple of times. While it may appear to be a simple piece of narration, there are some sophisticated writing techniques at work here, combined with a real variety of theatrical demands. Try to divide the speech up into different types of language. When is it description? When is it action? When is it setting mood? When is it dialogue? For example:

Descriptive narrative	It was no more than once upon a time when a poor woodcutter lived in a small house at the edge of a huge, dark forest. Now the woodcutter lived with his wife and his two young children – a boy called Hansel and a little girl called Gretel. It was hard enough for him to feed them all at the best of times.
Mood narrative	…but these were the worst of times; times of famine and hunger and starvation; and the woodcutter was lucky if he could get his hands on even a simple loaf of bread.
Action	Night after hungry night, he lay in his bed next to his thin wife, and he worried so much that he tossed and turned and he sighed and he mumbled and he moaned and he just couldn't sleep at all.

Dialogue in character	'Wife, wife, wife. What are we going to do? How can we feed our two poor children when we've hardly enough for ourselves? Wife, wife, what can be done?'
Mood narrative	As he fretted and sweated in the darkness, back came the bony voice of his wife; a voice as fierce as famine.

After you have identified these areas, think about how best to differentiate between them. Try to use your voice and body to help communicate the different language demands. For example:

➢ Be still and speak directly to the audience during the narrative lines

➢ Give action and movement to the words that you consider to be describing actions

➢ Change the tone and tension in your voice to emphasise words of mood

➢ Change your body shape physically when speaking as character, and find a voice that is different from your neutral narrative voice to create the person you represent.

Using these simple ideas to manage the language of the play will help you differentiate between the role you play as narrator and the role you play as character. This is the key to success in exploration and rehearsal of this text.

Creating a performance style

The action and events of the stories proceed quickly and jump from one location to another. The narrators and characters appear and disappear seamlessly, often being one and the same actor. You and your company must learn to tackle these problems quickly using simple but clear physical theatre storytelling techniques.

 Look at the opening of 'The Lady and the Lion' from 'A merchant was about to go…' to '… and she was delighted to see that he'd brought her a rose.'

Read through the text and then try to block the story, with the actors playing the parts and the rest of the company creating the locations and atmosphere. You will have to recognise the physical demands of this part of the story and create:

➢ The three daughters – representing their demands and what that tells us about them in terms of their greed

➢ The merchant's journey and his search for the jewels

➢ The forest

➢ A castle with a garden that has flowers on one side and snow on the other

➢ A rose bush

➢ A lion

➢ The journey home.

Tips Does this sound tricky? Here are some suggestions on how you might accomplish this:

➢ The characters should be created though use of voice and clear body posture and perhaps the use of a costume.

➢ A journey can be created simply by having the merchant walking on the spot and the company moving in the opposite direction – from left to right or from front to back – to create the theatrical illusion that the merchant is moving.

➢ The jewel could be hidden in boxes, under stones, behind walls, all created by the company.

➢ A sculpture of bodies intertwined like an old gnarled forest could easily be formed.

➢ The castle could be shaped with people as walls and turrets and perhaps a table or chairs to give levels. Flowers could be represented with hands, using finger movement and sound effects to convey the sense of falling snow.

➢ A rose bush could be created by all of the company's arms.

Working in this style can be great fun but it takes focused energy and can be very tiring. The trick in applying physical work is choosing the right time to create the image or movement. It must not detract from the words or fight with them for attention. The image or movement should not pre-empt the words either, but must allow itself to be cued by them, so that the audience can recognise both and then match them together.

Timing

When you are working though this exercise try to decide the best time to set up each of the images or movements and be specific and accurate about where they happen each time.

Mood

Each of the dramatised tales has a mood and a message of its own. Within each tale there lies a complex journey of moods and atmospheres. Your style of performance needs to capture and exploit this. We have talked briefly about how lighting can support and create mood in an earlier section but the protagonist in creating mood will be you as an actor and your company. You have all the tools necessary to control mood. For example, in addition to providing a variety of ways of speaking the text, your voice can also become an instrument. This type of text gives you wonderful opportunities to make soundscapes.

Your body, the bodies of your company and the space in which you work are not only vehicles for narration and for creating the characters but can also be the creators of the set and props, and through stylised movement can indicate the mood and intent of the action.

Read the section in 'Hansel and Gretel' from when the children first see the witch's house ('When it was midday…') up to 'This will make a tasty morsel for me to swallow'. Consider the section in terms of its potential for using soundscaping and movement to create mood.

Try some of the following:

➢ Build a soundscape of birds to imply the idyllic country scene when the house is first seen, using harmonic sounds and whistling.

➢ Build a creepy, menacing soundtrack to underscore the entry of the witch using a high-pitched humming.

➢ Create a sudden sound to support the sudden opening of the door in order to scare the audience upon the entry of the witch.

There is no specific stage direction or compulsion to do anything at any time. This type of text gives you the freedom to explore and create. You must look for opportunities to exploit and create dynamic moments. This what the examiner will be looking for.

➤ Use slow motion and exaggerated movement to show the witch taking the children by the hand and leading them into the house in order to build tension and emphasise that something is not right.

➤ Use a tableau or freeze of the witch standing over the children as they sleep to show her evil intent when she speaks her final lines in this section.

Physicalising and vocalising

Physicalising the text

As a character you will need to depict the range of characters you play clearly with appropriate movement and mannerisms. When/if acting as a narrator, you will need to communicate the story and the mood clearly with gesture and body language. As a member of the ensemble you will need to use your body and the space to support the location, staging and mood of the tales you are telling.

Vocalising the text

As a character you will need to depict the range of characters you play clearly with an appropriate and sustained accent or characterisation. As a narrator you will need to communicate the story and the mood clearly with a range of vocal states such as lyrical, harsh, staccato, flexible or mannered. As a member of the ensemble you will need to use your voice to support the location, staging and mood of the tales you are telling through creating soundscapes, soundtracks and sound effects.

Communication

A text like *Grimm Tales* gives you wonderful opportunities through physical and vocal work to show creative, sustained and focused communication and it is therefore an ideal text for this unit. You must be clear, however, about the intent of the piece, and be able to communicate to an audience a clear understanding of why the stories were written. This notion of communication is centred on your interpretation of the text, and will be conveyed through your use of space, staging, costumes, lighting and props as well as your actual performance.

A really good performance for this unit understands the intent of the text and brings new meaning to it by considering all aspects of its potential performance. *Grimm Tales* give great theatrical opportunity, but the theatrical **intent** of the text is to keep things clear and simple.

Text in Context

What do I have to do?

This unit is the final assessment for the AS year. Although it is a written paper to be sat under timed exam conditions, it should be seen as a chance to share and celebrate all the knowledge and experience that you have built up over the course. The questions in the exam will only ask you about things that you have experienced or thought about during the course and should be seen as a real opportunity to evaluate these experiences.

The whole of this unit should be thought of as a positive opportunity to show the examiner the thought-processes and work you have been involved in and have seen. In many ways, it really isn't an exam you need be anxious about because it is very much about you. It is also an exam you can thoroughly prepare for, in terms of your thinking, and you can even take your thinking into the exam in the form of structured notes: ten A4 pages of Context Summary Notes and ten A4 pages of Performance Analysis Notes.

What will the exam entail?

The unit is examined in a two-hour written exam, which is made up of two parts. Section A is concerned with the play that you performed for your unit 2 production. Section B is concerned with the live productions and plays that you have seen during the course. Each section will be broken down into three questions: you should spend about an hour on each section and about 20 minutes on each question. You may be expected to use diagrams and drawings at times to support and explain your answer.

 Although there will be three questions in Section B, you must write on only ONE live production. You cannot choose to write about more than one production or use the questions to talk about different productions. You must focus on one live production only.

Both Section A and Section B are broken down into three questions, because this unit aims to get you to think in three different ways about both the play that you were involved in and the play that you saw.

Three questions

You need to be able to:

➤ Analyse how characters, narrative and ideas are conveyed through theatre

➤ Recognise the contribution made to a piece of theatre by directors, designers and performers

➤ Understand the social, cultural and historical background of a play text, and how it demonstrates its relevance to its audience.

If this seems a little confusing at this stage then think about the three areas like this:

Interpreting the play text

How do we make meaning in theatre?

What choices does the director, designer or actor have when bringing the play text alive from the page to the stage?

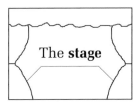

Performing the play

What are the conventions of staging and what are the tools of the actor?

The **audience**

Reaching the audience

How is a play made relevant to its audience?

Preparation

Even though this unit is a written paper sat under exam conditions, it is a student-friendly exam. Remember that you are allowed to take structured notes into the exam room. Therefore the key to success in this unit is PREPARATION. This is a unit that you can prepare for thoroughly and create support notes for. Anxiety and nerves can be alleviated to some degree by spending time thinking – both throughout your unit 2 work and before the exam – and preparing useful structured notes.

Section A

The difficulty with this element of the exam is that you cannot fully prepare yourself until you have performed the play. The performance could take place early in the spring term or possibly as late as mid May. However, the key to doing well in this section is to have the exam in the forefront of your mind when working on your production: although they are separate units and examined differently, you need to be thinking about the written exam throughout the performance process. It is therefore vital that you spend time organising your thoughts during the rehearsal process, making notes on key decisions that were made or problems that occurred. Practical details including alternative solutions will be vital when pulling together your examination notes.

Below, we try to give as much general advice as possible, but we draw upon the two play texts discussed in the Text in Performance chapter to give you some concrete examples. Again, don't worry if you haven't been looking at either of these specific plays: the advice here can be easily adapted to help you with whatever text you have chosen.

Getting started

As you approach this section you should have the following information available to you:

➤ A script of your unit 2 play that reflects the dialogue and action you presented. If you made cuts or edits then the script should have these.

➤ The script should also be annotated to show what you did for each page, unit, scene or moment. These annotations could be words, arrows, illustrations or whatever helped you rehearse and perform the piece.

➤ You should have a log of what you did in each session or rehearsal. This log should explain what you did and how you did it in terms of staging, as well as comment on why you did it and what you were trying to achieve or say to the audience.

➤ You should have a heading for each session/rehearsal which reflects what you were trying to do for that rehearsal, with an evaluation of whether you achieved it or not and why.

Reshaping your notes

The next few pages will lead you through the first stages of the process of preparing for the written examination. You need to rewrite your notes under the following headings, using the suggestions and questions to help. To give specific examples so that you can see what we mean by each of the headings, we have referred to the plays looked at in this guide for unit 2: *Blue Remembered Hills* and *Grimm Tales*. Using our approach, consider your own chosen play and think about how to adapt our points to it.

Plot

You will already be familiar with the story but is important that you condense the action of the play into key points of detail. Try each of the following activities as a way of improving your command of the plot.

 Summarise the main action of the play in two clear sentences. Only include essential information, but make sure that someone who is unfamiliar with the play would be able to understand what you have written.

There are 29 scenes in *Blue Remembered Hills* and they imply several different settings. Condense this information into the key points of action. Use punchy phrases similar to newspaper headlines as a way of summarising the content. If you feel you need more information, use smaller phrases or subheadings to aid your memory. Try to use vocabulary that will help you in the exam. For example, Scenes 1 and 2 might be summarised: 'Peter uses physical aggression to steal Willie's apple', with the additional headline of 'Boys remain friends'.

If you are studying an episodic play text like *Grimm Tales*, one really good way of remembering the plot is by marking the important moments with illustrations:

➤ Arrange the key moments of the stories into a numbered sequence

➤ Give each moment a title and a sentence that sums it up

➤ Then think of the action and how it would have looked to the audience

The selection of these moments is very important in making this exercise clear: you could end up with hundreds of pictures for every different movement on stage, and this is not helpful. Choose moments that are visually important. Remember that the drawings do not have to be totally accurate: they are there to remind you of what happened.

> ➤ Then try to draw between four and eight matchstick-men pictures from the perspective of the audience that indicate the basic stage positions of the characters and how the set and staging supported the action
> ➤ Underneath each of your drawings create a sentence that reminds you of the action of the episode.

Two examples might be:

Picture one

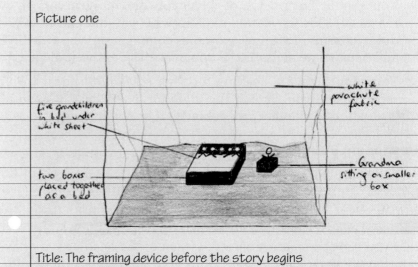

Title: The framing device before the story begins
Sentence: This is before the play text actually begins and was the way we introduced the story to the audience.
The action: Grandma is reading a book to her children. They want a scary story and so Grandma begins to tell them the story of 'Hansel and Gretel'.

Picture two

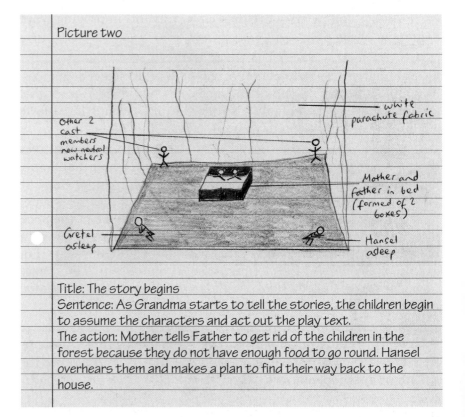

Title: The story begins
Sentence: As Grandma starts to tell the stories, the children begin to assume the characters and act out the play text.
The action: Mother tells Father to get rid of the children in the forest because they do not have enough food to go round. Hansel overhears them and makes a plan to find their way back to the house.

Themes and issues

When searching for themes and issues within a play, there is a danger that your thoughts may become slightly forced or that some ideas may be exaggerated in attempt to justify an interpretation.

Initially, keep your ideas simple. Reflect on what has struck you about the play and try to find different examples from the text or your rehearsal that might illustrate your points. Remember, themes are rarely straightforward, so do not worry at this stage if you appear to contradict yourself when you focus on different elements.

When tackling a question on themes, on cultural or historic influences, or on how you tried to make your play relevant to your audience, it may help you to think in the following terms:

1. WHO wrote the play, WHEN was it written and WHY was it written? Finding out about these things may help you understand more about the themes and issues within the play.

2. How did you try to make the play relevant to your audience in the way that you staged it? In other words, WHAT were you trying to say through the play, HOW did you do that and WHY?

Go back to your pictures illustrating the plot. If you have left enough space, ask yourself what, how and why as detailed *above*. For example:

> Picture one
> Title: The framing device before the story begins
> WHAT: We were trying to show the importance of storytelling and the power of the stories, as well as allowing the audience to see that the production was going to be a series of theatrically told tales.
> HOW: We used a framing device, in which a Grandma was putting her grandchildren to bed with the aid of bedtime stories. As Grandma tells the stories, the children act them out.
> WHY: We wanted the audience to be aware that the play was rooted in the art of storytelling. From a historical perspective, the Brothers Grimm originally collected the stories from an oral tradition, and we wanted the staging of the play to be true to this. This meant that the audience always knew they were seeing a story within a story. This in turn liberated their imagination, so that we could use the set and props to represent a whole range of things.

> Picture two
> Title: The story begins
> WHAT: We were showing how the family related to each other in this scene.
> HOW: The simple and symbolic set represented the relationships. The Mother and Father slept on one big bed and were thus able to be intimate and contrive the plan to kill the children. Hansel and Gretel were separated and slept on the floor, indicating their isolation.
> WHY: We wanted to show the apparent harmony of the parents and the isolation of the children, which would be reversed later in the story. From a social and cultural perspective, the presentation of the parents' attitude to the children had a very modern relevance to contemporary news stories concerning the abuse of children and we wanted to evoke this. From a historical perspective, the story of Hansel and Gretel very much reflects the childhood of the Brothers Grimm, who lost their father when they were very young and their mother when they were both students. It was their dedication to each other that brought them through their grief. This is very much like the resolution of 'Hansel and Gretel'.

Tip

Using an A3 sheet of paper, produce a collage that identifies the themes and issues presented in the play. Look at images from magazines, headlines from newspapers and quotations that comment on any of the ideas explored in the text.

Character

If you have chosen to perform a play that, like *Grimm Tales*, requires actors to take on multiple roles, you will need to identify the different roles you played in your production. Draw a simple sketch of yourself in the different guises you assumed. Give each guise a title and then try to describe the demands made upon you in that role. For example:

As both the Mother and the Witch, I had to define them clearly with use of voice and movement. I used a basic costume as Narrator and then added simple costume to represent my characters: the Mother had an apron, the Witch had a shawl, a hat and a pair of gloves with extended fingernails to indicate her cruelty. I used a sweet, sycophantic tone when addressing the children when trying to be nice, and a harsh, clipped, cruel voice to show my darker side. I tried to keep a straight body posture for the Mother and became much more twisted and bent when representing the Witch.

The characters of *Blue Remembered Hills* should be portrayed in such a way as to represent different images of childhood. Each of the seven roles is unique and as a group you should have looked carefully at creating seven very different roles that complement each other within the ensemble scenes: balance and range are needed in order to maintain your audience's interest.

Your Context Summary Notes should include a general overview of the decisions your group made about the portrayal of the characters. For example, in *Blue Remembered Hills* you should state how movement, voice and facial expressions were altered in order to convey a sense of age. You need to explain why you made these decisions and what they achieved rather than simply explaining what you did. These comments need to be supported with more detailed references to specific scenes, looking at how you used acting skills in order to create mood and atmosphere. Consider how you reacted with others: how did your use of eye contact and stage space convey the relationship between characters?

Identify any decisions that were made about status and how each character's role in the group altered as the play developed. Make sure these points are supported by practical examples rather than page references.

As with preparing your Exploration Notes, in your Context Summary Notes you should be aware of the structure of the play. In *Blue Remembered Hills*, for example, the action happens in chronological order and the acting style is essentially realistic, despite the obvious fact that children are played by adults. Scene length varies significantly with regular cutting between locations, reflecting the fact that it was originally written for television. Look at why some scenes are longer or shorter than the others. Why might this be structurally important?

Blue Remembered Hills has quite a slow, relaxed pace to it, which reflects the setting of a long summer holiday in 1943. Characters appear to stumble across each other; meetings are often by chance, implying the lack of purpose in their lives. Although several different locations are used, the scenes are structured so that the barn remains permanently in the audience's focus. Consider how this is done.

Structure

Identifying the important stages and watershed moments of rehearsal will be very important in responding appropriately to one of the types of question in the exam. Revisit your rehearsal log and try to isolate the vital moments of the process: where decisions were made, ideas rejected, alternatives considered and so on.

In rehearsal, you should have approached the play in three phases. Try to use these phases to give examples of the decisions you made concerning the set, staging, other design elements and characterisation. For example, if you looked at *Grimm Tales*, your notes might look like this:

Rehearsal process

> Phase one – early exploration
> This was time set aside to work on the style of staging. This was done early and took the shape of exploring the adapted stories. Time was also set aside here to think about and explore framing the stories within a context.
> Important because: It was during this time that we introduced elements of staging, props and costume, and also experimented with voices, bodies and the space. We also made final decisions about casting.
>
> Phase two – tackling the tales
> This was the heart of the rehearsal process, where the actual text was read, blocked and staged.
> Important because: It was during this phase that we: explored the narration, the characters and their dialogue; helped each other understand the intent of the scene and the themes and issues we were dealing with; began to detail the blocking in order for an audience to engage with the work and enjoy and understand the story.
>
> Phase three – polish and performance
> This was the final phase where we began to glue the stories together and saw the relationship between them and all their characters.
> Important because: It was a time to make sure we had one play rather than many, and to really secure the design elements of the performance such as lighting and sound.

Tip

In order to make your notes really useful here, you need to find **specific** examples from your rehearsal that back up the points you are making.

Intent

Although the direction of your production was probably led or supported by your teacher, you must still understand what the vision for the play was and, most importantly, what the play was trying to say. This notion can be understood as the directorial aim, or Ruling Idea. It is the concept that has been decided for the interpretation of the text, concerned with where the play is set, when it is set, how it looks and how it will be staged. Most importantly, it is concerned with WHY the production takes the shape it does and what it is attempting to convey to an audience.

Try to distance yourself from the play and ask yourself: if you were a member of the audience, how would you feel/what would you think at the end of the performance? Then ask yourself: how did you want your audience to feel at the end of the performance? Do these ideas match?

A production of *Grimm Tales* staged as recommended in the Text in Performance chapter of this guide and as discussed here in this chapter is probably trying to do three things:

1. Root the style of theatre in the storytelling tradition – whereby the emphasis is not on a sense of reality, but on the relationship with the audience and the audience's imagination – through the words of the story and simple staging.

2. Bring out modern relevance of stories that were in their own time cautionary tales, by relating them to contemporary news items and issues, such as child cruelty, child abduction, relationships between parents and children, greed, friendship and war.

3. Make reference to the story-tellers themselves, the Brothers Grimm, by alluding to the time of the original stories through costume and through an understanding of their reasons for collecting and recording them.

The audience should thus leave having been entertained through the theatricality of the production. They should also feel that there are messages for them concerning the way they live their lives and treat others. They should also think about why these stories were originally collected, and how they relate to current perceptions of our treatment of children, friends, parents and other nations.

In *Blue Remembered Hills*, Potter carefully manipulates the audience's response, taking them on the same childlike journey that the characters experience. The opening of the play should invite the audience to reflect on their own youth and the times when they played by themselves. By the end, he has cleverly undermined this initial image with a harsher vision of childhood and all its cruelty. Not only does the play warn against the glorification of the past, but also, ironically, its use of adult actors seems to comment on similar childish behaviour in older generations.

In your notes, examine the directorial aim for *Blue Remembered Hills* set out by your teacher. Look at whether this reinforces, alters or even contradicts Potter's vision. Focus on specific moments where the insecurities of characters may have been emphasised, or

Further reading

There is a useful section on the work of the director and textual analysis in *Drama and Theatre Studies at AS/ A Level* by Jonothan Neelands and Warwick Dobson (Hodder Arnold 2000).

perhaps on how you carefully staged images of childhood in order to create a certain mood or atmosphere.

Making your notes relevant

Once you have addressed each of the areas above, it is important to organise your thoughts into generic headings that will help you to prepare for specific responses. Although you are unlikely to be asked to answer a question simply on the role of the director, designer or performer – the focus will be on specific aspects of the rehearsal or performance – the areas below will provide a foundation for your ideas.

Once again, use these points as a guide. Have your existing notes beside you and make sure any relevant ideas are included in your final draft. Do not copy questions into your notes; you do not want to be distracted by other questions in the exam. Write down your response to the different points.

1. Director

Some of the questions may ask you to consider how your piece evolved in relation to the directorial aim or director's concept and it is therefore important that you see the director as someone who helped to shape the material rather than as someone who simply made sure all scenes were rehearsed.

Your teacher will have decided on a specific concept and you should identify this at the start of your notes, along with any key themes or issues that have been focused on during the process. You also need to think about and note down how the play relates to a modern audience. These ideas will be a useful starting point for certain questions, since they will not only enable you to identify what you were trying to achieve but also to evaluate the success of the final performance.

Having said this, it is important not to limit your directing notes to the work led by staff. Once you understand their vision then you can refer to how you personally interpreted the ideas through your rehearsals. Use the following areas as a prompt for your notes on the process. If you cannot think of any examples from your piece, ask the other actors and designers who were involved.

What conventions were used?

A convention is an unwritten rule used by the cast to create the world of the play. *Blue Remembered Hills*, for example, requires a range of locations: were these created in detail or implied through the convention of mime? Did certain corners of the stage imply the barn? Did the person with the highest status always carry a stick? Did certain exits imply that characters were heading towards the barn? Were blackouts used only when there was a clear sense of time passing? Think about *why* things were done in the way they were. What impact or effects did each element achieve? What would have happened if you had chosen to do it differently?

Key moments of rehearsal

Identify key moments of rehearsal when the directing really helped to shape the piece. This may focus on some of the exercises shown on pages 8–17 and 94 or other times when you felt the piece made real progress. Development is the key. Make sure you can identify the problem you were encountering, the directorial input and the effect this had. For example, for *Blue Remembered Hills* your notes might read:

> Fight between Peter and John. Difficult to stage. Early attempts too comic – undermined tension. Director looked at ten stages of fight. Director sculpted images. Headlock, leg grab. Focused on John's growing power. Successful but lacked some fluency between the different stages.

Relationships between characters

What decisions were made about the relationships between characters and how they should interact with each other? You may include generic phrases that apply to all relationships, or you could focus on specific decisions that were made about how two or three characters responded to each other. This could include references to the text, but always make sure you say how ideas were implemented during rehearsal and discuss the intended impact.

Interpretation of dialogue

In addition to general comments during rehearsals, specific attention may have been paid to the vocal work in a few scenes. For example, if you studied *Blue Remembered Hills* you may have looked closely at the range of tones used by Peter in the barn with Donald, or how the children's fear is vocally expressed in the last scene in the field. Give specific examples of advice you were given on tone, pace, pause, inflection and the intention behind the words. How did you want the audience to react?

Transition between scenes

Did your production have constant changes in scenes, as in *Blue Remembered Hills*? If so, the play could become quite fragmented. What advice was given in order to ensure smooth transitions from one scene to the next? Was music used and did you rehearse with it? How were entrances and exits choreographed? What were you trying to achieve in each case? Or was your play composed of a series of stories, like *Grimm Tales*? If so, did you require a framing device to play an important role in linking the narratives together and indicating to the audience the themes and issues within them? How did you construct this framing, and were there alternative ways you could have achieved the same result?

Cutting and shaping

Since the piece shouldn't exceed the one-hour time limit, did you have to cut any scenes or stories? If so, why did you choose to leave out certain material? How was the whole piece shaped in order to ensure a range in emotions, pace and so on? Think about the difficulties the format of the piece posed and how they were dealt with effectively.

Staging scenes

Consider the phrase 'staging scenes' in the widest sense rather than simply in terms of audience position and set. Consider how each of the scenes was created within the space in order to have a specific impact on the audience. Think about alternative ways this could have been done: why did you think what you did was most effective?

In your notes, remember to back up general points with specific examples. Take this list of points concerning the staging of *Grimm*

Tales as a guide. This will help you to focus your answer and score well in the exam.

General points:
- We didn't want to create a naturalistic set because we felt that it would be too limiting. The set needed to be flexible because a number of stories were being told within it.
- We didn't want to create a sophisticated or complicated set because we wanted to reflect the simplicity and clarity of the storytelling through our set.
- We used the framing device to define what set and props could be used.
- We wanted to keep the space open and flexible to force the audience to use their imagination.
- We wanted the audience to see us creating the illusion of theatre through representative props.
- We wanted to keep the space as open as possible, allowing the company to use it to create movement sequences and to use their bodies to create the physical imagery, allowing for simple and quick-paced storytelling.

Specific examples:
In 'Hansel and Gretel', we used two large wooden trunks and a smaller box. Firstly, the trunks were the bed in which the children slept in the framing device. We then made them in to:
- The bed in which the Mother and Father slept by placing them together
- Staging to support the creation of the forest with actors standing on them
- The house made of food, by placing them on top of each other
- The cell and the oven by placing them on the short side and using the lids as doors
- The duck that crosses the stream by putting them together and having the actors become the head, wings and tail
- Hansel and Gretel's house on their return by placing them together on their short sides.

2. Designer

It may be that you or another member of your group has chosen to specialise in one of the design options. If this is the case, you should have specific details about the choices that were made and the intended impact. Talk to the individuals responsible and glean as much information as you can about what was done and why.

On the other hand, if the decisions have been made by either your teacher or the group as a whole, then it is important that you find time to discuss and understand the design decisions that have been made and the reasons behind them. Remember, you may be asked to evaluate the choices that were made, so make sure you have considered alternative designs in your notes. Be ready to comment on staging, costume, lighting and sound.

Where were the audience positioned? How big was the performance space? What set was used? Give details about the size, colour, shape, and texture. What did it represent or symbolise? How might the audience react when they enter the space? How could it have been improved? Were props used or were they

Look at the advice given on pages 89–91 for students designing for *Blue Remembered Hills* and on pages 104–108 for *Grimm Tales*.

Staging the play

mimed? How did this help or hinder rehearsal and performance? See *above* for more on staging decisions.

Costume

How did costume convey a sense of period? How were colour, style and material used to create character? Did the manner in which the costumes were worn affect the audience's understanding? Did you achieve what you intended to here? Were aspects of the performance affected by the designs chosen? Did they allow for the physical nature of some of the scenes?

For example, your notes for *Blue Remembered Hills* might read:

> John. Quite formal. White shirt, light grey tank-top, dark grey shorts. Neat and ordered costume reflects personality. Feels most comfortable when in control. Allowed free movement in fight with Peter. Shirt became untucked. Ceremoniously tucks back in at end of scene. Copied by Willie who has switched allegiance.

Lighting

A cross fade is a change from one lighting state to another.

Was the lighting minimal or did it actively help to convey the mood of the piece? Make notes on the colours used, the speed of any cross fades, the intensity or brightness of different lights, when blackouts were used (if at all), the position of lanterns and any specific effects that were used to create a sense of location. For example, for *Grimm Tales* you might write:

> General points:
> - We used a very simple lighting design for the production to complement the simplicity of the storytelling technique.
> - We used two cover states: a white one to represent the story within the frame and a more yellow one to show that the story was being told and acted out.
> - We used blue washes and red washes to indicate changes in mood and time
> - We used a front floor flood to create shadows and create an atmosphere of evil and tension by casting large shadows on the back wall.
>
> Specific points:
> - A natural white general was used in the opening framing sequence when Grandma was telling the stories, just to present this scene as an actual story.
> - A yellow general was cross-faded as Grandma started to tell the stories and the children became the actors involved in the stories, to indicate that the production was moving out of the framing device and into the story within the story.
> - A blue wash was used to indicate night in the house, and also the spooky forest.
> - The red wash was used as an effect whenever the oven was opened and when the Witch was finally thrown in, to indicate the heat.
> - The floor flood was used on the initial entry of the Witch to heighten the tension of her entry and to show her evil side as a shadow cast on the wall.

Remember, however, always to go on to link each of your points to an **intended impact** and assess whether you felt it was successful.

Sound

List each of the effects that were used. What choices were made concerning the positioning of speakers, the volume of the effects and the timing with the action on stage? Were they successful during performance? Was music or any other sound effect used to create each new scene? What instruments were used? Try to describe it in terms that someone unfamiliar to your production could imagine. Did this help to sustain the mood and atmosphere of the production? Would you change any of the sounds used?

The Samuel French edition (1984) of *Blue Remembered Hills* includes a full lighting plot, effects plot and a furniture and property list.

3. Performer

If you have acted in the production, then you will have a wide variety of experiences on which to draw in this section. However, you must be careful not simply to list ideas that you have explored. You must select the most relevant experiences that will help you to answer the specific focus of the question.

In addition to understanding your own role, it is important that you have information on the work of at least two of the other performers in your group. This will allow you to answer a question that requires you to look at three different characters.

Many of your notes will be personal to your experience of the play. The decisions you made, the problems you encountered and the solutions that were offered should all relate to your journey through the rehearsal process.

Factual information

Begin with the given circumstances for each of your three chosen characters. These can be brief quotations from the text or short phrases compiled by you or the director that summarise their portrayal. Give practical details as to how these traits were realised in performance, referring to voice, movement and facial expression.

How the portrayal altered

Clearly you will have gone on to adapt your initial views on the character. Try to identify when you altered your perception. How did you change your performance? Did it evolve during your work on a specific scene or during a run-through? Why were the changes made? How might it influence the audience's perception of your character? Does this reflect the director's aim?

Key rehearsals

Identify at least three moments that really helped you to improve the portrayal of your character. It could relate to off-text improvisation, to advice you were given or even to something that happened by accident. Explain how your work improved, giving precise references to the changes you made and stating why you felt this made the performance more successful.

Problematic scenes

Each member of your group will have found certain scenes difficult to portray successfully. It may be that they struggled with dialogue, felt awkward with their movement or found it hard to identify with the emotion. Choose three problems and explain what action was taken in order to overcome them. State how the portrayal had improved.

Interaction with others

How did your character relate to the other characters you have selected? In addition to the lines spoken to each other, how were looks, gestures, pause and proximity to one another used to convey a sense of their relationship? Why did you decide to do it in this way?

Ensemble work

See the notes on characterisation in *Grimm Tales* on pages 110–111.

If you chose to study a piece of ensemble physical theatre like *Grimm Tales*, you may find that you will have less to say about the emotional demands of becoming one particular character and more on the demands of being part of an ensemble. You may need to discuss, for example, the problems encountered when switching from character to neutral narrator to part of the ensemble – and all the changes in voice patterns and physical representation that this entailed. How did you overcome these? What effect do you think these constant changes had on the audience?

Research

What research did you undertake in order to help you create a more convincing character? If you watched the BBC film of *Blue Remembered Hills*, what did you learn from the performances? If you observed seven-year-olds, give specific examples of how they move and speak. Did you talk to anyone about their experiences of being a child during the second world war? What observations did they make about friendships and the games played? How did this help you?

Themes and issues

In rehearsing either of our example plays, you should have reflected on your own experiences as a child. You may be the sort of person who dotes on younger relations and even yearns for the apparent simplicity of your early years. Has rehearsing the play made you aware that you are guilty of glorifying the past? Have you been reminded how fragile and threatening childhood can be? In a wider sense, have you reflected on how violence permeates society and on whether it is wrong to accept such behaviour, either towards children or among them? When making notes on these issues, guard against an overly sincere response that lacks personal reflection. Think about the themes explored and assess whether your viewpoint has changed.

Answering questions

It is useful to spend some time thinking about the three different types of question you can expect to encounter in this part of the exam.

Tip

You may prefer to organise your Context Summary Notes in terms of these themes, rather than under the headings of director, designer, performer.

1. How meaning is made in **performance**.
    How is the story told in performance? How is the space used to tell the story? How are the characters presented? How is the play staged? You will need to consider: WHAT you performed to make meaning; HOW you did it, with examples of actual scenes and moments; WHY you did it that way and what alternative approaches you could have adopted.

2. How decisions and choices are made in the process of **interpretation**.
    How did you, the director and the designer bring meaning to the play? What decisions and choices did you make in terms of the interpretation of the play? How did the play look on the page, and what did it then look like on the stage? You need to focus on WHAT decisions and choices you made on the journey through rehearsal to production, looking at WHY you made those choices and WHAT alternative interpretations you might have examined.

3. How the text is made **relevant** to its audience.
What were the social, historical and cultural influences on this production? How was it made relevant to its audience? What was the production trying to say? You will need to consider HOW an audience receives meaning through the space, the set, the staging of the play and the characters, and WHAT they do and say.

Exam technique

Read through all the questions before you begin writing. This will help to ensure that you can provide a balanced response over each of the questions, giving your strongest answers without worrying about repeating yourself in what you perceive to be similar questions. Once you have chosen your questions, highlight the key words that are the focus of this particular question. Students often skim-read a question and assume they understand it, but be careful. Look at the specific words used. Think carefully about the information you have in your notes and how it can support your answer.

It is important that you aim to spend equal time on each question. Longer answers that use up too much time will be self-penalising. Three good responses will often be awarded more marks overall than one excellent response and two average ones. If a question appears easy and you have plenty to say, this might be an opportunity to save time. If you can write quickly and cover all of the points, then use the valuable minutes on a harder question rather than giving a longer response. You should aim to give a balanced answer: if a question asks for a specific number of examples to illustrate your ideas then make sure you give adequate detail for each area. If there is no such guidance, always give two or three well-developed ideas.

You know approximately what the examiner is going to ask you in this exam. But the questions will be worded in such a way as to make you think carefully about the productions you have been involved in and respond spontaneously on the day to the specific words of the question. The key is not to be thrown. The question you will see on the exam paper will not mention your production by name, nor will it refer to specific scenes or characters by name, because the question obviously has to be relevant to all the students who have been involved in a range of different productions.

Bear in mind also that the questions will fall into two different types: general questions about the whole performance, where you can choose examples from anywhere within your production; and specific questions about moments or scenes, where you must choose your examples from that part of the production.

Structure each part of your answer in the form of point, evidence and analysis:

Point: This is the key issue(s) you are focusing on in a particular paragraph. It could be a key scene, theme, design concept or character trait.

Getting started

> Don't go in to the exam with prepared answers, or you will fall in to the common trap of repeating an answer that you've previously written in a practice essay: make sure you're answering what the question actually asks rather than what you'd like it to be asking.

Time management

The question

Structuring your answer

Evidence: This is your opportunity to respond with practical examples from your own experience. It can be appropriate to use SHORT extracts from your text, but remember that the focus should be on your practical understanding.

Analysis: This allows you to focus on why decisions were made. You may consider their impact on the actors or the audience. You should also focus on alternatives. What other ideas did you reject? On reflection, what other interpretations could have been more successful?

The time pressure in this examination is quite tight and success therefore depends on your ability to address the demands of each question in a focused and organised manner.

Below are three different questions covering different areas of the rehearsal and performing process. Read each stage and try to complete the different exercises before you begin the next section. Do not skim-read this section; allow yourself proper time to tackle each idea.

 Sample question 1 (Blue Remembered Hills)

> <u>Describe</u> how <u>directorial decisions</u> helped to create the <u>mood</u> and <u>atmosphere</u> necessary for your production.

 Understanding the question

When you read the question in the exam, it is vital that you focus on the specific areas that are raised. Students often assume the question says something they have seen before and then begin writing an answer that they wrote for a mock examination. This is extremely dangerous and can easily result in a candidate writing a very weak response when they are clearly capable of doing much better.

➤ Look carefully at the question above and the demands it makes. Once you have read the question, it can be very useful to underline the key words. This helps you to focus on what you are being asked to do and to make sure that you do not miss any elements of the question in your answer.

➤ The focus is on directorial decisions and you should therefore look at the notes you have made about the role of the director.

➤ Identify the mood and atmosphere that needed to be created in your piece. Remember that this is unlikely to remain constant so you should consider a range of examples.

➤ You are asked to describe the choices made, although in doing so you should always look to evaluate their success.

➤ Where possible, try to offer alternatives to the decisions the director made. This would demonstrate a strong understanding of the play and show that you are actively involved in the process.

Tip

Try to use appropriate technical vocabulary. Always make sure that you are using it in a relevant context, however, and not just arbitrarily sprinkling your answers with theatrical words.

Your director will have a ruling idea, which should govern all decisions made about the piece. Make sure this is contained within your notes and refer to it in this answer.

Planning your response

During this half of the exam, you are recommended to spend one hour answering three questions, which equates to 20 minutes per question. This is extremely tight and you must resist any temptation to spend longer on one answer since this will ultimately have a negative effect on the other responses.

Before you begin answering, take a moment to organise your thoughts. You are not expected to write a fluent and intelligently structured essay, but chaotic thoughts will often prevent an insightful answer.

 Write down the key scenes in the play where you think a strong mood and atmosphere were created by the directorial decisions made. Make brief notes on how this was done. Your list might look something like this:

> Willie's entrance. Scene 1. The magic of childhood. Nostalgic. Audience in round. Music - flute, clarinet and violins at fast pace. Playful. Innocent. Whole performance space. Childlike giggles. Wide eyes.
>
> Peter and Donald in the barn. Two victims. A sense of optimism combined with moments of aggression. Confined space. Peter's threats emphasised by his use of space, climbing on set. Donald initially small and low. Peter admires Donald's jam jar scam. Excited giggle.
>
> Donald burning in barn. Fear and lost innocence. Actors divided by imaginary barn wall. The panic in faces. Loud sound effect. Red floor light. Peter last to leave.

These notes address three different scenes, giving you approximately five minutes per scene. When you are practising essay writing, try to focus on three different areas. The exam board will never ask for more and at times will specify fewer.

 Writing your response

Before you address the question, write the play and the playwright at the top of your paper. This will make it immediately clear to the examiner which text you are focusing on. You do not need to write a formal introduction, but a sentence that identifies your approach to the question can help.

> In our production, the director aimed to create a sense of nostalgia as the audience reflected on their own childhood while reminding them how cruel children can be and the consequences of their violence.

Once you have done this you should aim to spend equal time on each paragraph identifying HOW mood and atmosphere were created and WHY. These two words are vital. You must focus on specific directorial decisions and how they were implemented. How did Willie enter? How were actors positioned? How were lines delivered? Follow each of these with a clear understanding of

Remember to offer alternatives, for example: 'Although facing the barn emphasised the fear of the children, not all of the audience could see their faces. It could have been more effective if the children turned to each other in desperation, allowing different groups of the audience to see their expressions and imagine the panic they are experiencing.'

why these decisions were made. Why did he enter from the corner at fast pace? Why did Peter stand above Donald on the hay bail? Why were the lines shouted at the imaginary door of the barn?

Sample question 2 (Blue Remembered Hills)

Explain how the <u>portrayal</u> of <u>two</u> of the play's <u>characters</u> was influenced by the <u>set design</u>.

Once again, when planning your response, you must begin by focusing on the specific nature of the question. **Two** characters need to be discussed. Choose these carefully since you will need to relate your response to how the actors used the space. Depending on the complexity of your staging, you may choose to focus on two contrasting performances, or instead you could identify which characters use the set in the most interesting way.

The question asks you to identify how the portrayal was influenced by the set and therefore implies a relationship between these two elements. You may choose to focus on how each of two roles was altered because of the demands of the set or indeed how the design was changed to accommodate each actor's needs. Whatever your focus, you should aim to give a sense of the process of creating both the set and the characters in order to communicate the aims of the piece successfully.

Look at the following response carefully and try to evaluate how successfully the writer addresses the question:

> A good tight opening. The student focuses on the demands of the question, outlining the method of staging and the reasons for choosing these two roles.

Our performance was staged in the round, in an intimate theatre space. The stage was approximately six metres square, and key pieces of set were used to represent both the barn and the large expanse of fields implied in the stage directions. The two roles most influenced by the demands of the design were Willie and Donald, since the characters were at times solely responsible for creating the location.

> Although we get a sense that a clear directorial decision has been made, this explanation isn't clear. What colours were used? How did he stand? Why was this important at the start of the play?

In each of the corners, large white screens were positioned to act as cycloramas. These were lit by different colours at different times to indicate changes in location. As Willie entered he stood in front of one of the screens to show he was in a field. We spent a lot of time working on how he stood, as it would be important for the audience to understand where he was.

> A much better paragraph, which conveys a real sense of progression and a link between set and acting. Although the initial part of the response focuses on an imagined set and therefore lacks design detail, the development of the design and the effect it has on characterisation clearly answers the question.

The director felt it was important for Willie's entrance to capture the playful spirit of children during long summer holidays. The actor was told to imagine he was walking on stepping-stones through a stream as he moved diagonally from one corner of the stage to the other. He raised his arms to balance while making large strides and fixing his stare on each imaginary stone. The idea was fun to watch but seemed slightly false and was different from the memories I have of my childhood. The actor seemed to be focusing more on creating the stream than his character and he lost the sense of age. However, the set was adapted to include short, fat logs approximately 30 centimetres in height instead of pretend stones. This not only helped to create the sense of the wood for the audience but the real stumps became fun to walk on and the actor playing Willie experimented with a range of different childlike leaps and moments of imbalance which were hilarious to watch.

The corner of the stage that represented the barn was the only place where the audience sees Donald and we felt it was important that it reflected his character. A tired-looking, misshapen hay bail was positioned across the corner and several old wooden farming tools that have been forgotten about were hung from the screen, which was always lit in a reddish-brown colour.

> This is an interesting attempt to show how the set reflects one of the characters. There clearly is a sense of a link between design and characterisation but a greater sense of portrayal is needed. The ideas are implied but they need to be more explicit.

The logs, which ran diagonally across the stage, represented the walls of the barn suggesting that Donald is trapped within the space just as the audience is trapped within the round staging. The actor highlighted this by the way he approached the imaginary window and stared out, focusing his eyes on a distant image, almost longing for the courage to leave the safety of his barn. The bail of straw was to be Donald's comfort and, in rehearsal, time was spent working with how the actor might sit on it, hug it and even stroke it as if it was a living creature, something that understood him. This relationship could have further highlighted his inability to bond with real children if he had run to the straw for safety when Audrey, Angela and Peter teased him.

> The paragraph begins with a good link between character and audience, implying the intended impact of the staging. This is followed with clear practical examples that show how actor and set work to convey meaning. Alternatives are also offered as to how an idea could be further developed.

Sample question 3 (Grimm Tales)

How did the form and structure of the play influence your Unit 2 presentation?

Try to answer this yourself under timed conditions. Here are some suggestions on how to approach the question:

Firstly, you need to consider WHAT the form and structure of the play you're studying is. For example, what is the content of the play, how is it put together and how it is told? You would need to refer to the separate stories, the episodic nature of the stories and the simple storytelling style in which they are written.

For each aspect of the form and structure you mention, you need to discuss HOW you presented this element of the play and then justify WHY this aspect of the form and structure led you to present the play in the way you did. Think about:

➢ The set and space
➢ The movement
➢ The ensemble
➢ The actors
➢ Characterisation
➢ The framing device (if you used one).

Try to give a suggestion of alternatives to show the process of choices and to explain why you chose the option you did.

Section B: Live theatre analysis

Getting started

You may be misled if you think that this section is just about writing reviews of plays you have seen. Reading reviews in

Reading reviews

broadsheet newspapers or magazines will, of course, ultimately help you to understand the nature of theatre criticism and will improve your literary and theatrical vocabulary. However, it will not necessarily directly help you to analyse the making of meaning in theatre, as this unit demands. Reviews can be too concerned with judgements about good and bad. This unit is concerned with understanding what makes effective meaning in the theatre.

What to see

In this section you will be required to answer **three** questions on **one live production** that you have visited and seen. However, this does not prevent you from seeing many different productions. It would be highly beneficial in terms of developing your understanding of theatre if you were able to see a range of different pieces of theatre during your year of study. Try to see at least three or four different types of theatre. You could break theatre down into a number of simple genres and try to see:

➢ A serious play

➢ A musical play

➢ A Shakespeare play

➢ A comedy.

Going to the theatre obviously depends very much on where you live, what is available and also how much ticket prices are. So remember that you can see amateur work as well as professional work – and this means the work of students and your school. Choosing to evaluate your annual school production or that of another school can be just as valuable as analysing professional theatre. Also be aware that you must see a live production – you cannot settle for writing about a play you have seen a recording of, or on television. The whole essence of this unit is the live interaction between a production and its audience.

> You could even choose to analyse the unit 2 work of another group in your year – it just cannot be the performance that you yourself took part in, as this is obviously covered in Section A of this unit.

Whatever you choose to see and ultimately choose to write about must give you opportunity to analyse and evaluate, in a way that is enthusiastic and positive, and yet critical. It must offer you the potential to:

➢ Evaluate how characters, narrative and ideas were conveyed through the performance

➢ Recognise the contribution made to the theatrical experience by directors, designers and performers

➢ Apply a knowledge and understanding of the social, cultural and historical background of the play.

A good choice of play in performance will really help you respond to the key aspects the examiners look for in the unit, and will enable you to shape a series of good answers.

Where to start

Understanding how to break down a piece of live theatre into areas that you can write about can begin before you even enter the theatre, and can be part of a gradual process of thinking. In fact you may not realise it, but you have already begun that process. The whole AS course is designed to get you thinking about how theatre is made and why it is made in particular ways. In your unit 1 study you looked at different types of play texts and explored how to perform them practically, and in your notes you tried to justify the decisions you made. In your unit 2 performance you took a play text and made decisions as director, designer and actor as to how to bring the text to life on stage and make it relevant to your audience. This section is simply asking you to look at the process of taking a play and putting it on the stage, and to try to understand what the choices and decisions were for those who were involved in that process. It's as simple as that.

An argument to bear in mind at all times is the idea that **everything in theatre is deliberate, nothing is accidental**. This means that conscious decisions are made and applied to everything, from the lighting through to the characterisation – everything you see and hear in a performance has been deliberately created in order to make meaning. It is for us as an audience to work out the signs and symbols, and to discover the messages of the play.

Getting practice

Although you must write about a live performance in your written exam, it can be good introductory practice to begin honing your analytical skills on a recorded production.

Try to get hold of a copy on VHS or DVD of the new stage production of *Jesus Christ Superstar* by the Really Useful Company. The musical traces the last few days of Jesus (through the eyes of Judas) as he tries to preach, and is arrested, tried and finally crucified.

Before you start watching the film, try to write down some thoughts about what you might already know about the story. Think about the story under the following headings: location, time/period, action/events, characters, themes and issues.

Now watch the production. As you do so, write down some observations about the following areas:

What did the set look like? Write about how different areas were suggested and what the set reminded you of from the way it looked.

How was it staged? Think about how the action moved about in the set and how events were staged within it.

How did the characters look? Think about how you thought the characters would look and how they were portrayed through the choice of actor.

How was it costumed? Talk about different groups of people, lead characters and anything that the costumes or props reminded you of from the way they looked.

How was it lit? Try to uncover examples of how the lighting creates effects, moods or atmospheres that might inform us of a place, special event or even create symbolic meaning.

Here are some very good, detailed responses to the headings above, to give you an idea of what you should be looking for when making your rough notes:

Set

The original events took place in ancient Israel and the set captured this through the way it reflected Roman architecture in form, shape and colour. It also appeared modern through use of scaffolding and graffiti, which makes you think about modern Palestine and Israel and the state of affairs in that part of the world today. The set hints back to its original time but also brings new relevance and meaning to its audience by talking about the struggle that exists today. In Jesus' time it was the Romans suppressing the Jews but now it is the Jews in conflict with the Palestinians.

Staging

The set and the space are used to represent many things. The space is defined by the action within it, by the lighting used, by the characters populating the space and by the words that are sung which tell us where we are. The same spaces are used many times, but it doesn't matter as we are willing to accept that they are different locations. The architecture of the set, the use of levels and the different forms of stylised movement within the space all help to create the mood and meaning of the scenes.

Characters

The cast and lead roles are multicultural and this would not have been the case in the original story. The multicultural cast does many things to the story. It reminds us that this is a piece of theatre and not a reality: the message and the story thus become important rather than just the individuals within it. It makes the story relevant to all of us and not just the country or nation that the story originally existed within. And it makes the story have modern meaning, in that it could be about people today in any kind of political or warlike struggle.

Costumes and props

There is an eclectic mix of costumes: traditional robes and garments of the original period, but also modern combat gear and modern dress among the disciples. The Romans had hints of the original period in their uniforms, but were also wearing costumes that were a reminder of Nazi Germany through their colour, cut and insignia. The priests and Jews also wore garments that reminded me of propaganda that was used to incite anti-Semitic feelings in the 1930s. This mix of costumes that hints to various periods manages to: root the production in its original time, make reference to periods in history when the Jews were repressed, and also bring the story right into the modern world, with reference to modern-day conflicts and terrorism. The use of modern weapons as well as spears and swords also supports this intention.

Lighting

The lighting is a mix of mood and effect. In order to bring religious and spiritual significance to Jesus, the lighting on him is often enhanced with a bright white effect. Mood and atmosphere are often created with intensity and colour. The location of each scene is also denoted with angled lighting to show if the scene is outside or inside, but often to give the impression of many buildings, windows and doors in a busy yet broken-down city.

Intent   What do you think the director wanted you to come away thinking about having seen this production? Was he concerned about historical detail or who the real Jesus was? Was he more interested in showing that the struggle against oppression and the fight for freedom still goes on in other guises? Try to write a statement that describes what you think the production was trying to say to the audience about the story of Jesus and Judas.

You should be able to see from this practice exercise that decisions have been made with careful consideration of the text by the director, designers and performers in order to make this production relevant and thought-provoking to a modern audience.

Interpretation

If all productions of the same play were identical, theatre would be very dull and boring. It would soon lead to definitive versions that could be videoed and simply watched on television. The performance would not be able to take into consideration changes in theatre trends, performance styles, new actors bringing new approaches to parts, cultural changes, historical events and news, social injustices or events. Theatre is a live and living art form that reflects the here and now. The possibility of bringing new meaning to any play, or making the audience view it with new eyes and ears, through the process of interpretation, is what keeps theatre alive.

In this section, it is your task to explore WHAT decisions have been made regarding the play texts, HOW they have been put into the production and WHY they have been made.

Performance Analysis Notes

Since you will not be seeing the production and then taking the exam the next day, it is really important that you make extensive and detailed notes on each of the productions you visit in order to make them as fresh as possible when you enter the exam room. As we have already stated, you are permitted to take in up to ten sides of A4 in notes to this exam. Try to use the guidelines below to help you begin to shape your notes.

Pre-show expectations

Begin your thinking about the production before you even get to the theatre.

The theatre: Is this a theatre you have visited before? Do you know anything about the layout of the theatre, the relationship between the stage and the audience, the size of theatre, where you will be sitting?

The play: Is this a play you know? Have you seen it before? Have you read it? Do you have an idea of how it might look already?

The company: Who is performing the play? Has this company been brought together just to perform this play or is it a repertory company that has done other plays together? How long have they been performing this play?

The poster: Does the poster give any clues about the content of the play, the issues the play is dealing with, the style in which the play is being performed? There may be symbols on the poster that give you information or hints about how the play will be interpreted or how themes may be revealed.

Further study

Try the above exercise again and see if you can begin to read the signs of interpretation that are used. Look at Baz Luhrmann's *Romeo and Juliet*, with Leonardo DiCaprio. Consider the same heading, but this time don't just observe what is done – try to make the leap and decide WHY you think these decisions have been made.

The relationships between audience and the stage, between you and the play text, and between members of the company are all important factors that may affect the impact of the performance on you.

In the theatre

Try to understand and assess the stage layout. There are various traditional stage layouts, all of which have different relationships with the audience and suit different types of theatre. Make sure you have read and understood the descriptions and diagrams of the different types of stage layout featured on pages 32–36 of this guide before you go.

Many modern productions may be touring and are often at the mercy of the space that they are visiting. A production may work in the intimate space originally designed for it but may then not work very well when it visits a large proscenium arch theatre on its tour. Its effectiveness as a production may often come down to the relationship between the acting space and where the audience is sitting.

Check where you are sitting and try to work out what the layout of the theatre is, using the descriptions on pages 32–36 as a starting point. With this in mind, consider how the use of space affects your relationship with the play. Draw the layout so that you can remember this point.

Space and layout

An example of this is *The Blue Room*, originally produced at the Donmar Theatre in London with Nicole Kidman. The play relies on the intimacy of the relationships and the believability of the characters created. This play worked beautifully in the intimate thrust layout of the small Donmar Theatre where the audience could almost reach out and touch the electricity between performers. The play was then re-worked and toured large theatres all over Britain in an end-on layout, and the intimacy was arguably lost.

The programme

Some programmes can be very expensive and may only include colour photographs of the show: these will not be helpful. A good programme may hold a director's or designer's statement, or an interview with an actor, or some background contextual information about the play and when it was written. All of these will help considerably when it comes to making notes.

The programme will also have a cast list and this will be vital when it comes to making notes on the performances of the actors and the characters they created. You must refer to the actors, NOT the characters in your exam response.

Exam board

The programme will also hold the basic details of the production, which are essential to you. The first thing you will need to do in the exam is to write down the **title** of the play, the **date** you saw it, and **where** you saw it. Remember though that you cannot take the programme into your exam.

During the play

Set

As the show begins, spend some initial time thinking about the set. Remember that all of the set may not be revealed immediately and it may change considerably during the show as scenes and locations change. Try to ask yourself some basic questions about the set as it is revealed to you at the beginning:

➢ How does the set actually create or define the performance space?

➢ Does the set suggest a location or various locations and how does it do that?

➢ Does the set suggest a time or period in which the action is set and how does it do that?

➢ How does the set's use of exits, entrances and levels help the action of the play?

➢ Does the set suggest or create a world for the characters to live in?

➢ Is this world created in a literal or naturalistic set, or does the set use other ideas and symbols to suggest the world of the play?

➢ Does the set suggest or contribute towards a mood by using shapes, colours, materials, scale or distortion?

➢ Does the set suggest or create any clues about the themes and issues or meaning of the play through use of symbols?

If you know the play of the production you are visiting, try to think how the actual play text describes the setting of the action of the play, or if it offers up any suggestions as to how this should be realised in the set. Does the production adhere to the guidelines provided in the text, or has the designer chosen to ignore them completely? If so, what does this tell you about the company's interpretation of the play?

Try to think about the set under two headings:

Function: What does the set need in order to be able to fulfil the requirements of the action? The play text may demand certain things such as exits and entrances, levels and specific locations. How does the set in the production you have seen serve these basic functional requirements?

Symbol: What does the set suggest or create that is extra to what is written in the play text? A designer will make decisions and choices in conjunction with the director regarding the themes and action of the play. These decisions and choices will affect the whole concept of the set. The set can create moods, suggest themes and support staging styles just through the way the space is defined, the objects and shapes chosen, its use of materials, its use of colours, its use of textures, and its use of scale and proportion.

It can be a naturalistic set trying to evoke a real world or it can be an abstract set trying to suggest an impression of a world.

How would you describe the set of the production you have seen, and is it trying to suggest meaning? Soon after seeing the production, draw some plans and illustrations of the set so that you will be able to remember it clearly later. Draw a downward-looking plan and indicate where and what the scenic elements are. Then draw a 3D impression of the set looking at the stage from the point of view of the audience.

> Some texts, such as Arthur Miller's *The Crucible*, offer detailed instructions as to the creation of the set, right down to detail concerning the colour and textures of the doors and windows. Some, such as Shakespeare's plays, offer very little.

Web link

> The National Theatre put on a production of *An Inspector Calls* in which the text's description of an Edwardian living room was ignored in favour of a more surreal setting. For images of this production, see www.costume.org/ travel/1999uktour/disk29/ MVC-011f.jpg and www.churchilltheatre.co.uk/ spring6.html.

Staging

The staging concerns the way in which the story is told and the way in which characters move within the set. This is linked to the concepts of form and structure you will have explored for unit 1.

The staging of the production will be dependent on:

➤ The **genre** of the production: is it a musical, a comedy, a play trying to show modern reality, for example?

➤ The **content** of the play text: is it about love, war, the supernatural, for example?

➤ The way in which it is **written**: the words on the page and how the characters are created will affect the way it can be performed.

➤ The **response** that the production is trying to get from the audience: is it trying to make the audience think, feel, laugh, cry?

From your previous study in unit 1, you probably already have a basic grasp of some of the choices concerning staging and the way in which they can be applied to the play text:

See pages 8–17 for more on Stanislavski.

Stanislavski emphasised a very naturalistic way of staging plays, in which the action of the play was realistic and the characters would speak, move and behave in a style that would mirror reality and make the audience confront their own emotions. Does the production you are watching feel like it's trying to echo reality? Do the characters speak and move realistically? Do you feel as though you are watching a slice of real life, whether in modern times or the past? Do you feel engaged emotionally with the action and characters of the play?

See pages 17–24 for more on Brecht.

Brecht explored a way of presenting drama with epic and universal themes through a variety of theatre conventions that forced the audience to think about the stories they were watching and listening to. Does the production you are watching feel like a grand and epic story? Do the actors play a number of characters and can you see them changing from one costume to another in order to represent these characters? Do the actors use song to make comment on the action or to move the action along? Do the characters speak directly to you in the audience as well as each other?

See pages 24–32 for more on Artaud.

Artaud tried to change the relationship between the performance and the audience. He wanted to invent a new language of total theatre that involved changing the performance space, redefining the way actors communicate through language and movement, and trying to shake and shock the audience into having a cathartic experience rather than being passive spectators. Does the production you are watching seem to challenge the way in which the audience and the action relate? Do the movement and language used in the production seem unique or special in the way that they tell the story? Does the way in which the events are presented shake or shock you?

Web links

There are of course many other major influences in terms of staging. Try using the Internet to find out more about:

Steven Berkoff's physical theatre
www.east-productions.demon.co.uk
www.iainfisher.com/berkoff.html

Jerzy Grotowski's poor theatre
www.owendaly.com/jeff/grotdir.htm
www.geocities.com/akatsavou/grotovski_en.html

Pinter's and Beckett's theatre of the absurd
www2.arts.gla.ac.uk/Slavonic/Absurd.htm
http://dana.ucc.nau.edu/~sek5/classpage.html
http://vzone.virgin.net/numb.world/rhino.absurd.htm

The history of staging
www.win.net/~kudzu/history.html
www.videoccasions-nw.com/history/theatrer.html

The influence of world theatre
www.csuohio.edu/history/japan/japan12.html
http://marian.creighton.edu/~marian-w/academics/english/japan/kabuki/kabuki2.html

What is essential to your understanding and appreciation of staging is that in modern theatrical productions, directors draw on a huge vocabulary of ideas, and can mix and match staging forms and conventions. Equally, the beauty of modern theatre is that the resources and ideas for staging are no longer simply held within the history of theatre – modern directors are using the influences of pop music videos, cinema, rock concerts and all sorts of other modern media to find ways of staging theatrical ideas.

When discussing staging styles in this section, do not hesitate to refer to practitioners, other plays you have seen or more modern references to films or pop videos. The production you are watching may well have been inspired or influenced in such a way.

The lighting that supports performances can be very obvious – for example in support of a big show such as Ben Elton's musical *We Will Rock You* – or subtle and almost unnoticeable – for example in support of Elton's play *Popcorn*, which takes place primarily in a living room.

The primary function of lighting is to allow the audience to see the action and characters of the play. In some productions this is all that is necessary or indeed required. Brecht, for example, often used normal house lighting in his plays because he did not want the lighting to detract or distract from the simple telling of the story: lighting can create a magical world and Brecht preferred his audiences to be reminded of their own, real world. Brecht's denial of theatrical lighting was an acknowledgement of its power, and he made a deliberate choice not to use it.

The lighting of a play can have a number of different purposes:

It can create meaning by itself...
➢ By defining a location on stage quickly by focusing on one area. The use of fading to black and then up again can indicate different locations, as can cross-fading between different areas and levels on the stage. Location can also be indicated through use of a gobo, which can project a specific sense of location such as forest branches, city skylines or a church window.

➢ Lighting can define time – and changes in time – through fades. It can indicate a time of day by using colour and intensity of light.

➢ Lighting can show a change in season through altering colour and intensity.

➢ Lighting can be used to confront, blind and/or shock the audience for a particular reason.

It can support the meaning made by the set...
➢ Lighting can be directly linked to a source on stage, such as a lamp or a candle in the set.

➢ Lighting can be used to indicate sources of light through windows and doors to support the time, location and mood of the set.

➢ Lighting can be used on a cyclorama to give an indication of epic, large-scale location, or time of day.

Web link

The French-Canadian director Robert Lepage uses cinematic imagery and technology in his productions to explore new meanings and new relevancies for his audiences. He is in conversation with a past director of the National Theatre at www.nationaltheatre.org.uk/?lid=2627

Lighting

It can create its own mood, atmosphere and tension...

➤ Lighting can create a mood and atmosphere through different types of colour and levels of intensity.

➤ Lighting can use certain angles and directions to create sinister mood and scary atmospheres.

➤ Lighting can use filtering effects and join with smoke to create an ambience and specific tension.

It can create symbolic meaning...

➤ Lighting can use angle, colour, intensity and effect to create symbols in support of the action of the play. A simple use of a red gel, for example, may support an act of murder or of rage.

➤ A simple use of a floor flood facing a character could create a huge shadow on the back wall or cyclorama to indicate a growth in that character's ego or a giant metaphorical presence on stage.

When you are watching your productions, try consciously to examine the use of lighting and decide whether it fits into any of the categories explored above. Above all, be aware that the lighting represents a series of deliberate choices made in support of the play.

Write down the different uses of lighting in the show you've seen and give a specific example of when it was done, how it was done and why you think it was done. If possible, illustrate the example with a drawing.

Sound

Sound can work in a very similar way to the lighting, in that it can help indicate time and location through chosen effects and soundtracks. It can also create mood and atmosphere. Cinema has shown how important sound can be in creating tension at certain points of a story, and how important music and song can be in heightening feelings and bringing an emotional intensity to a moment or scene.

Sound and music have a number of different uses. They can create a **location**, such as a busy street or the country, through use of selected sound effects. They can support the events of a scene by creating a soundtrack to underscore the **action** and create mood. They can heighten the emotional **intensity** of a scene by using an evocative or poignant sound, melody or song.

Sound can also be used to **comment** on the action. Using sound that is in **contrast** to the action of the scene can make the audience think about what is going on and why. It can move the action forward by reflecting the passing of time in some way. It can also create symbolic meaning, in that sounds, chanting or music could precede or accompany an event to give it a symbolic significance. A good example of this is in *Equus*, in which the ritualistic sound and chanting are very much a part of the overall concept of the play, with its themes concerning religion and sex.

See page 43 for more on *Equus*.

Dont worry if you are confused by any of this – it will become clearer in the next section as we look at a specific example of a play in analysis.

Costume

Different types of plays will give different types of opportunity for costumes. However, whether the play is set in modern Britain or Elizabethan England, whether it is naturalistic or abstract in staging, the costumes will have been designed or chosen to reflect a number of things.

➢ They will be a part of an overall concept which begins with the director's and designer's ideas for the interpretation of the play text, continues with the development of this directorial aim or Ruling Idea and is eventually manifest in the set and staging of the play

➢ They will reflect and support the character or characters that wear them

➢ They will suggest a period and location

➢ They could suggest or support the themes being explored.

See page 120 for more on this.

The degree to which the costume does the above really depends on the type of production you are seeing and how much scope there is for interpretation. When observing costume, look for obvious signs of character representation, location and period representation, but also examine colour, shape, texture and material to see what is being suggested about the person who wears it.

Also be aware that costume and the way it is used can indicate the style of staging of the play. If actors are playing many roles and thus using costume to represent the characters they are embodying, then the costume takes on extra significance, because it becomes the character. The way that the audience identifies that character is through the costume.

For example, a king could be represented only by a crown. The character of the king never changes, but the actors playing him do. In this instance, the costume is the audience's sign of recognition for that character, and the costume itself becomes the representation of the character.

Props

The properties used within a play can be thought of in a number of clear ways. They too can support the location and period of the play in a very literal sense: a gramophone in a living room will give a sense of a specific period in time. They can also have a symbolic value: the gramophone, for example, may also represent memories of the past for one of the characters through its music, and thus become a symbol of their past.

Equally, props can have significance if placed ironically within a production. Our gramophone could be placed in a modern setting, where it would stand out, forcing the audience to think about what point the director might be trying to make.

Props can also have a representational value in terms of being many things within a production. The gramophone could be used as a hearing aid; it may become a witch's hat, a beautiful shell on a beach, a weapon. The way in which a prop is used will give you many clues as to the style of the production. And, as with costume, props can be key signs as to how to recognise characters. Props such as handbags, hats and walking sticks can be used to help actors create characters and help the audience identify them.

Think carefully about what props are used in the production you are watching and how they are used. Do they have a value greater than what they literally are? Not all props will carry this value but some may. Describe WHEN, HOW and WHY the props are used and use illustration if possible.

The performances

The characters within a play often carry the story, and their actions and words are what draw us into the events of the production. It can be very difficult to distance yourself from the characters to try to decide WHAT the actor is doing, HOW they are doing it and most importantly, WHY they are doing it. It is very important that you avoid making value judgements on the performance, such as 'He was very good' or 'I didn't like her'. You need to address what the actor was doing and whether it was effective.

Key questions　A really good way to start thinking about an actor's performance is to break it down into clear questions:

> ➤ What did the actor do with their voice to create the character?

> ➤ How did the actor move to create their character?

> ➤ What did the actor look like in creating their character?

> ➤ How did the actor relate to the other actors and the space in creating their character?

> ➤ Did the actor make you feel anything for their character?

> ➤ Did the actor make you think about anything through the way they created the character?

These questions force you to regard the actor separately from the character. They also force you to consider the performance in distinct sections, under which we can begin to build supplementary questions to aid our analysis of the performance. Consider the more detailed questions in the table below:

Voice	Could you hear what the actor was saying? Did the actor use an accent or a dialect? Was the characterisation sustained throughout the play? How would you describe the voice of the character? Was it soft/loud, gentle/harsh, natural/mannered? Did it change during certain scenes? Did you feel that the voice was always appropriate to the moment or action?
Movement	Was gesture and body language used effectively? What type of movement did the style of production or the character demand? Was the movement appropriate to the character and to the moment or scene? Did the character's movement change during the course of the play for any reason? Did the actor use any props in their creation of the character and how did these affect movement?
Costume	What was the costume of the character? Did the costume change and for what reasons? Did the costume represent anything or give you clues to the style, themes or meaning of the play? What were the textures and colours of the costume?
Relationships	How did the actor relate to the other actors or characters on the stage? Did you feel that the actor had any real engagement with the other actors? How did the actor use the space to communicate their character? How did the actor relate to or communicate with the audience?

Audience response: emotions	How did the actor's performance make you feel?
	Were you moved at any point?
	Did you feel pity for, sympathy for or even empathy with the character at any point?
	Did you like them or hate them, and why?
	Think of a specific scene or moment when you were affected by a character's portrayal, and why.
	Did the style of acting affect the way you felt?
	Did you feel distanced or alienated from the character, or did you feel up close and personal?
Audience response: thoughts	Did the way in which the actor presented their character make you think about the story or themes of the play?
	Did the character make you think about what you might do or feel if you were in their position?
	Were you psychologically engaged, emotionally engaged or both? Note down any examples.

Can you think of any words or phrases that sum up the style of acting you witnessed? Try to relate these terms to the practitioners and concepts that you have already explored on the course.

Acting styles

You need to build a vocabulary of descriptors for acting styles. Make sure you are confident with what the following terms mean: naturalistic, believable, introspective, sensitive, reflective, stylised, physical, controlled, animated, intense, focused, calculated, demonstrative, declamatory, larger than life, stereotypical, melodramatic, mannered, indulgent, ineffectual, gimmicky.

Remember that simply making these observations and using these descriptions is not enough. You cannot just describe WHAT is being done; you must give examples from the production of HOW – by describing a scene, moment or event from the performance – and ultimately WHY they portrayed their character like this, by explaining their role in the overall interpretation and in terms of the directorial aim.

The interpretation

This is the journey from page to stage. In order for you to understand this journey fully, you need to have an awareness of what the play looked like as a text. It would be a good idea therefore to try to find a copy of the play text, read it, and consider what the stage directions and instructions tell you about how it should be raised on the stage. Do you think the performance does justice to the script? How was the performance different from your expectations?

Is there a Ruling Idea that comes out of the production through the concept and in the message and meaning? What do you think the director was trying to say about the play through the production? What was your overall response to it? Were there any significant moments or scenes? Did you recognise any influences from areas of theatre that you have already studied? Did you recognise any influences from any other cultural sources?

How would you describe what the production was trying to do?

Again, it would be good here to use a vocabulary of terms that you have come across in exploring other areas of the course: for example, you might describe the production as thought-provoking in the style of epic theatre, emotional in a naturalistic way or shocking in the vein of total theatre.

Alternatives

Further reading

Drama and Theatre Studies by Simon Cooper and Sally Mackay (Nelson Thornes 2000) offers up some excellent approaches to analysing performances. It also gives clear examples of performances that have been analysed.

Finally, bearing in mind that the journey of interpretation is all about decisions and choices, it is very important to consider what alternative choices the director could have made concerning the production. Try to find a couple of examples from the production where you think another approach, another set idea, another lighting idea or another element of performance could have been used.

Sample Performance Analysis Notes

You should now be equipped with a system of analysis that allows you to watch a production and begin to break it down, through the use of manageable questions under manageable headings. Let's look at some sample student notes on an actual performance in order to get a clear idea of how to put this into practice. Bear in mind that your notes do not have to resemble these exactly – you will probably want to include more sketches and pictures.

Blood Brothers the musical, written by Willy Russell and performed at the Phoenix Theatre, London.

Pre-show expectations
THEATRE: Knew very little about Phoenix Theatre, just that it was old Victorian theatre so could expect end on proscenium-arch layout with audience in stalls and circle.
PLAY: Had read play so knew it was piece of musical theatre about twins separated at birth and brought up in differing households in modern city setting.
COMPANY: Brought together specifically for this production. Linda Nolan, from pop group The Nolans, playing the central role of Mrs Johnstone – wasn't sure about pop singer playing lead role, thought it might prevent me concentrating on story.

Poster
• Two male hands locked together in a brotherly handshake. Background: cityscape with epic blood-red sky.
• What this told me: play will be about togetherness and love of two males; sense of significance of them being brothers.
• Cityscape located play for me – recognised building as one in Liverpool.
• Blood-red sky gave real sense of play's epic nature; also suggested it would be dealing with issues and themes even greater than the two hands locked together in the foreground.

The space and layout
• As anticipated: large Victorian theatre with wide stage and large seating capacity.
• Didn't feel that distant from the stage, as in second row of the stalls, but those in the audience further away may not have felt same intimacy.
• Seemed to be some compromise with the proscenium arch – stage jutted out past the arch into an apron in attempt to reach audience.
• These theatres originally intended to allow large audiences to enjoy spectacle of Victorian melodrama – fitted needs of Blood Brothers as epic story with spectacle and declamatory acting styles.

The programme
- Clear indication of cast of actors and parts they played.
- List of songs, their order, who sang them.
- Explanation of setting simply stated 'The play is set in Liverpool'. No detail of specific location or when it will happen or change.
- Two really interesting articles:
    1: By Willy Russell about how and why he wrote Blood Brothers. Gave insight into play's structure and use of songs. Built up expectation that it would try to use songs in a different way from normal musicals and attempt to be different in form and structure.
    2: About Liverpool and Willy Russell. Helped me realise tradition of writing, humour and music in Liverpool, and understand significance of placing the play specifically in Liverpool during 1950s to 1980s, and not just in any city or time period. Made me wonder whether Blood Brothers could work in any city setting.

The set
- Clearly defined PERFORMANCE SPACE. Stage surrounded on three sides by raised platform. Side platforms house band and musicians but were disguised as rows of houses. Back platform was walkway in form of iron bridge.
- Houses on stage right seemed run down and working class; houses on stage left seemed to give impression of being larger and grander.
- Large, flat floor space between platforms was raked but initially empty.
- Large backdrop showed cityscape similar to that on poster, indicated city location. Cyclorama backdrop also presented huge sky as shown in poster.
- Mrs Johnstone's home generally represented by area outside house and alleys around it.
- Mrs Lyons' home represented by bringing inside of house out into flat floor space, using flying false wall, carpet and various items of furniture.
- Two sides of houses suggested two different types of street: one very working-class and one more middle-class – SUPPORTED THEMES in story and different backgrounds of twins after separation.
- Combination of fixed set (defining space) and moveable set (working within fixed area) created own magic – made me think less about the literal quality of story and more about message behind it. Always aware that was piece of theatre – reminded me of Brecht.
- Use of levels and fixed set area allowing Narrator to roam and move effortlessly supported atmosphere of supernatural – promoted notion of superstition at heart of Mrs Johnstone's actions.
- Set suggested TIME PERIOD in not-too-distant past – architecture and style of houses suggested 1950s. BUT: action of play moves in time, tracing characters as they grow up – set dealt with this in number of ways: although basic platforms/houses remained same throughout, number of changes were indicated through other means – backdrop changed in second half, showing move to more rural setting outside city.
- Internal setting of the houses: brought out into the empty floor space between platforms on movable trucks and by using movable props.
- As time passed different items of furniture used.

- As LOCATION changed for Mrs Johnstone, a different internal setting was brought out – new kitchen. Showed improved social position.
- Large floor space used very inventively to show number of locations: different streets, beach, park. Moveable items brought on and off to give an indication of setting – bus, fun fair, various rooms, prison cell, town hall.
- Set provided whole range of exits and entrances and levels: really aided STAGING of play. Narrator (omnipresent and watching and commenting on the action) could use levels and alleys to keep appearing and disappearing, and to watch from a distance.
- Play's STRUCTURE made up of series of episodic scenes showing characters as through large number of years; pace and momentum really important. Set aided this: large floor space, many exits and entrances from it, and the levels around it allowed quick scene changes; could overlap scenes, one ending and disappearing off one way while another set up from another way – ensured momentum and engagement with audience.
- Set suggested world in which characters live, but didn't present it as a literal world. Style of play and passage of time during it demanded locations could be suggested through quickly changed sets, represented by lighting, props and words.
- Style of set in conjunction with staging made me very aware of production as piece of theatre – made me think about story being told rather than just lives of characters. Messages and themes became very universal – although story about people, began to take on epic status.
- Clearly met functional demands of play – provided clear definition of locations and provided space and levels for the action to flow freely and quickly.

The staging

- Some clear conventions and devices at work in production.
- Piece of theatre that has songs – all have particular role within production.
- Play spans 30 years, but same groups of actors play all parts/ages. Clearly named parts (Mrs Johnstone, Mickey, Eddie etc) play same part all the way through (so twins actors have to play twins at 7, 14, 28 onwards). Also multi-role – play number of parts, e.g. milkman, gynaecologist, bus conductor.
- Play begins with end: audience immediately realises that twins going to die but has no idea how that happens or why.
- Narrator provided to pass information directly to audience. Also makes comment on action of play and gets audience to think about what has happened and why.
- Locations suggested by props and moveable sets brought on and off by actors – audience fully aware they're involved in watching a story in a theatre. Familiar device from Brecht: concerned with confronting audience with themes and issues of paramount importance to society; even though play concerned with individuals, story concerned with larger, more universal messages.
- Blood Brothers very moving experience. Characters presented so that feel for them and sympathise with them as people as well as feel angry and upset by themes of play.
- Set allows staging to move quickly and sustain pace of play despite epic move through time and location.

The lighting

- Lighting played important part, as large open stage space became many different LOCATIONS very quickly – light helped define different locations by focusing audience's attention to certain areas of stage.
- Action moved quickly between two houses placed on stage right and stage left – supported by cross-fading lights.
- Audience's attention quickly changed to Narrator standing on raised platform at back by cross-fading light to him.
- Location also indicated by type of light: city scenes used more yellow, phosphorous lighting, often dimmed, gelled blue to indicate night time; country scenes much brighter, tried to create more natural light using straw-coloured gels.
- Simple gobo helped create size and atmosphere of prison cell.
- Lighting used to indicate passing of TIME by fading up and down accompanied by music and/or words.
- Lighting indicated changes in the time of the day with colour gels and changes in seasons by use of colour and angle.
- Lighting large cyclorama sometimes supported time of day/night, sometimes supported city/country location.
- Lighting used very much to create MOOD and tension. Cyclorama coloured in vast washes of blues and red to support supernatural feel of Narrator and to indicate superstition and sometimes hate being expressed on stage.
- When action in small rooms, cells or alley, lighting evoked mood and atmosphere through use of obtuse and interesting angles.
- When key action on stage that was part of themes and issues of play, lighting heightened moment by changing from natural light of room or location to more symbolic colour and sinister angle.
- Lighting also used in conjunction with songs and music: when action more stylised through use of song and movement, lighting changed from more natural light to more obvious light effect to support change of style.

The sound

- Sound very important contributor to both action and atmosphere. Very cinematic soundtrack: music for much of performance, supporting scenes, heightening mood and emotion; songs carried much of the narrative and commentary.
- Great deal of underscore – supported dialogue and heightened mood e.g. when children playing in park or when Sammy and Mickey were robbing local shop. Music integral part of mood creation.
- Narrator's role always supported by music. Role both inside and outside action of play; spooky music accompanied his appearances and generally gave warning that he was commentating on something bad happening in a prophetic way.
- SONGS like 'Marilyn Monroe' and music sequences like 'Forever 18' pushed action of the play forward and covered many years in lives of characters by passing information to audience.
- Songs like 'Shoes upon the table' made significant and effective comment on action and brought audience's attention to meaning of action.
- Songs like 'Easy Terms' and 'I'm Not Saying a Word' heightened emotion of scene and used melody and lyric to make audience feel something for characters.

- Music often introduced in action before or after song was sung – creating a motif that audience recognised. Narrator's music generally made audience aware of his entrance or that something significant was happening. Music from 'That Guy' heralded happening between Mickey and Eddie.
- So music took on very strong role and importance in itself and linked feelings, people and action to audience.

The costumes
- Costumes clearly indicated class and status – defined very clearly difference between Johnstone and Lyons families, from early childhood, through school years right up to ending when twins young men working.
- Also clearly indicated passing of time from 1950s to 1980s as reflected real fashion trends.
- Narrator's neutral, black, timeless suit gave him evil, haunting and supernatural presence.
- Costumes used to define the age developments in characters.
- Ensemble of actors used costumes to define different characters they were playing.

The props
- Props important in giving audience clear idea of location and setting of scenes.
- Simple furniture represented Mrs Lyons' middle-class home; washing-line represented poverty Mrs Johnstone faced.
- Benches quickly appeared and represented bus (rather than a whole bus appearing).
- Chairs represented seating in cinema.
- Table and chair represented cell.
- Gun: seemed to have metaphorical and symbolic value. Toy gun made significant early in play as the reason Mickey and Eddie become friends when playing Cowboys and Indians; Mickey, Eddie and Linda sneak off with Sammy's airgun to shoot at statue in park as their friendship develops; Eddie gives Mickey toy gun as parting present when leaving for the country; Mickey, Eddie and Linda shoot gun at fair as part of growing-up sequence; Mickey forced into using real gun by Sammy to earn much-needed money; Mickey shoots Eddie and is shot by police at end. Gun represents play, friendship, trouble and ultimately fate of both twins – pivotal prop.

> Choose central performances to think about for this section. You may be asked to write about more than one performance, so it would be useful to make notes on two characters. In *Blood Brothers* Mickey would be a good performance to consider in conjunction with either his twin Eddie or his mum Mrs Johnstone.

The performances: Mickey, played by Stephen Palfreman

Voice:
- Playing character at ages 7, 14, 18 and older is quite a challenge. Used his voice to great effect in representing different stages of his character.
- Dialect definitely rooted in Liverpool – gave real sense of location.
- Voice at 7 full of real enthusiasm and excitement. Had taken idea of innocence and fun and really exaggerated and animated his voice by using pace, volume and heightened tone to create a voice that was not trying to be realistically like a 7-year-old but give the impression of a 7-year-old.

- At 14: voice deepened, tried to be much more cool and sophisticated, but were moments when he was so excited it almost resorted back to 7-year-old's voice – showed his character still had enthusiasm and energy of a child.
- At 18: voice became measured and controlled. Struggling with own feelings and trying to understand the words around him – voice reflected that uncertainty.
- As older man: had gone through mental and emotional trauma – voice reflected time in prison and loss of dignity and self-worth. Almost resorted back to pace, volume and heightened tone of 7-year-old, but this time through pain, not excitement.

Movement:
- Physical gesture and movement were a really important part of the way the character was communicated in the different stages of his development.
- As 7-year-old: managed to communicate tension and pent-up energy that a 7-year-old has. Brought physical life to character through scratching and stretching of sleeveless jumper and use of invisible horse to move from one space to another.
- Some stereotypical observations communicated? Character was very much larger than life – but in context of the set, staging and size of space, character was effectively communicated and represented.
- 14-year-old: body language and posture much more laid-back – desire to be seen as cool, especially in context of relationship with Linda. Showed tension beneath cool exterior at times – explosions of physical action and gesticulation expressed frustration of character. This made for great comic effect.
- Actor showed real physical control as character developed through teens: body language and movement much more measured – reflected clearly the character maturing.
- As Mickey got involved in the robbery, spent time in prison and became unwell before leading to final showdown with Eddie, actor showed real physical regression to the pent-up energy and frustration of his early portrayal. This time nervous energy contained within character not waiting to burst out and play - this time it wanted to explode with anger and rage. This journey superbly handled and motivation behind the physicality clearly explained through music and dialogue.

Costume:
- Social status of Mickey at all ages clear from costumes; it contrasted well with costumes worn by twin brother Eddie.
- Clearly indicated location - e.g. school scene at 14, growing-up sequence, later in prison, and finally when working in factory.
- Costume at its most effective when showing ageing process - clearly defined periods of time that character passed through.
- Actor used costume very well in depicting his age and his mental state, e.g. punishment his ragged sleeveless jumper took when he was 7 showed his energy and frustration after his mother had told him off; way he played with his shorts after being released from prison showed fragility and insecurity of his mental state.

Relationships:
- Great feeling of ensemble within group of actors. Playing variety of roles helped build up ensemble feel and quickly made actors familiar to audience.

- Passing of time and development of characters also made them very familiar – shared their experiences of extreme happiness and sorrow.
- Nature of play and its inherent tragedy also seemed to bring company closer. Although certain characters were in relationships of animosity, there was real sense of reconciliation and respect at curtain call – lifted the play.
- All actors seemed very comfortable with each other and with space they were playing in – must be result of working together on play for extended period of time, but production didn't seem tired.

Personal response: emotions
- Stephen Palfreman's Mickey constantly made me feel emotional. At all stages in his age development the performance was getting response from me.
- As child: humour, but great poignancy as relationship with Eddie was built up only to be shattered by events outside Mickey's control.
- Early part of play was spent building relationship with audience through combination of great joy and happiness and then great sadness.
- It was Mickey who initially talked directly to audience when explaining about brother and family. In many respects, though mother tells the story, it is through his eyes that story is revealed and through him that we live events: our sympathy and emotional link is to him.
- Much of emotional attachment to Mickey was because he was victim of fate: could have been with Eddie if Eddie hadn't been given away, or could have been like Eddie and enjoyed comfort of financial security if he had been given away.
- Even when he suffers a nervous breakdown we still sympathise and share his agony because still victim of fate in tragic hero style.
- Sense of poignancy for audience made more extreme because know that ultimately Mickey will die – saw it at beginning.

Personal response: thoughts
- Also engaged by Mickey on psychological level.
- Share the story through him and begin to understand what he is thinking.
- Share his thoughts about Linda – wanting to love her but not being able to express that love.
- Share emotional breakdown and suspicions regarding Linda and Eddie.
- Understand what he means when cries out at end to mother 'Why couldn't you have given me away?'
- Mickey forces audience, even more than Narrator, to confront why things have happened and think about how we would have behaved in similar situation or how we could change his fate. Narrator merely passes comment upon them.

Acting styles
- Difficult to sum up acting style – seemed to be a mix of styles.
- Characters clearly defined and represented through costumes.
- Named characters larger than life and at times stereotypical; represented through clear use of voice and movement.
- Did not appear to be trying to be naturalistic – clear representation of age and type and at times spoke directly to audience.

- Did display whole range of emotional experiences – shared with audience who could sympathise and even empathise.
- Although characters were servants to wider story, we still cared very much about them.

The interpretation
- Production had very epic feel.
- Set spectacular; music and song brought a real grand spectacle to arguably simple story.
- Theatrical conventions made audience think about themes and issues of story.
- Ability to see band and mechanics of piece of theatre never detracted from story – in fact made story more powerful because always aware that it was story – made us think about 'what if it were true?'.
- Simple story about simple people but had much grander allusions. Felt like it was story about audience and society. Made audience really care about characters and action they were involved in, then sped us forward in time to next significant moment in their lives and immersed us in emotion of that moment.
- Story strikes clear chords and resonances with its audience: story about injustice, friendship and love – all themes mean something to all of us, are universal.
- Space and style of staging told me I was going to enjoy an epic piece of storytelling that would make me think. But because sat so close to stage and felt I was in intimate space, and because characters and story had touched something in me, felt I witnessed something both epic and very personal.

Answering questions

As with Section A, questions in this section will be grouped around three concepts. Refresh your memory on these:

1. **Performance**

    How did the actors create the characters?

    How did the characters tell the story of the play?

    Look at your notes on the actors' performances and how the production was staged, and be able to refer to how the set and technical elements helped tell the story.

2. **Interpretation**

    How did the director and designer bring meaning to the play?

    What decisions and choices did they make in their interpretation of the play?

    Look at the section of your notes that deals with how meaning is made and communicated in theatre – including your pre-show expectations, the set, the staging, the lighting, the sound, the costumes and the interpretation.

3. **Relevance**

    What were the social, historical or cultural influences on this production?

    How was it made relevant to its audience?

    What was the production trying to say?

    Look at the sections of your notes that are relevant to the way the production spoke to its audience. An audience receives meaning through the space itself, the set, the staging of the play, the characters and what they do and say.

Remember, when structuring your notes and in the exam, you need to employ the following process:

1. Be clear about WHAT you are saying. Clearly identify your point.

2. Be sure to describe HOW your point was achieved. Give a specific example from the action of the production for each of your points.

3. Be sure to explain WHY you have chosen this point. You must justify your answer with an explanation as to why the example was done in such a way and its importance to the production.

4. Finally, always consider ALTERNATIVES to what was done. Suggest another way that the characters could have been presented or the play staged, and explain why it was perhaps not done in that way. Remember that this question is about decisions and choices.